NARRATIVE

OF THE

LIFE AND TRAVELS

OF

SERJEANT B——.

WRITTEN BY HIMSELF.

"Call upon me in the day of trouble, I will deliver thee, and thou shalt glorify me."

"I shall not die, but live, and declare the works of the Lord."

EDINBURGH:
PRINTED FOR DAVID BROWN,
16, SOUTH ST. ANDREW'S STREET;
CHALMERS AND COLLINS, GLASGOW;
KNIGHT & LACEY, 24, PATERNOSTER-ROW,
LONDON.

1823.

ADVERTISEMENT.

In justice to the unpretending Author of this volume, it is necessary to notice that the idea of publishing it in no respect originated with himself. The circumstances which led to its appearance may be very briefly stated.

On the Serjeant's arrival in this country from India, he found himself surrounded by an extensive circle of relations, to which the excellence of his own character soon added many personal friends. As might be expected, the occurrences of his past life and travels, frequently formed the topics of conversation at their occasional meetings; and as he had from an early period, for his own amusement and edification, been in the habit of keeping an exact journal of all "the providences that befel him," he frequently had recourse to it for the purpose of aiding his recollection, and exhibiting more vividly the state of his feelings at various periods, and under the various incidents of his life. Many passages of the Journal excited a very pleasing and deep interest in those to whom they were communicated, and the desire of perusing it gradually extended itself to persons in a higher condition of life. A clergyman particularly, under whose pastoral care he was for some time placed, was so much struck with the interesting, as well as the instructive character of these "simple annals," that he urged the Author, in a very kind but pressing manner, to collect the more material passages in the original Journal into something like a continued narrative; and to transcribe them in a connected and legible form, for the private enjoyment of his particular friends. Our Author, to whom nothing is more agreeable than to have his mind or hands usefully occupied, undertook the task, and executed it with a degree of neatness, which would have done great credit to a more practised scribe. The manuscript volume was, of course, in very great request in his own neighbourhood, and was perused by none without peculiar pleasure; but, for several years, no idea of printing it presented itself to his own mind, though it was frequently suggested by those who had been permitted to read it. It lately fell into the hands of the writer of this notice, whose feelings in perusing it certainly were those of extreme delight; and finding that one or two friends, in whose judgment he placed the highest confidence, coincided with him in opinion, he strongly recommended to the Author that it should be published. His reluctance to this public appearance, was only overcome through the influence of a suggestion rising up in his own mind, that the work might not only perhaps afford pleasure and instruction, but that, should any profits arise from the sale, he would be enabled thereby to gratify his feelings, by devoting them to the support of Bible and Missionary Societies, or other pious purposes.

The task of the Editor, while the sheets were passing through the press, has been of a very limited kind, being chiefly confined to the correction of a few *glaring* errors in grammar or style, which the writer's very imperfect education necessarily occasioned. Though the most perfect liberty was conceded to him, the Editor felt no disposition to make any changes affecting that extreme naïveté and simplicity of style which appeared to form at least one peculiar and novel charm in the original narrative.

The Editor abstains from any attempt to characterize the volume, as he feels that, from peculiar circumstances, he has become too much enamoured of the Author and his performance, to possess the requisite coolness for doing the work strict justice.

He now sends it into the world, humbly trusting that the same kind Providence that watched over the Author, amid manifold perils, temptations, and afflictions, will furnish him with fresh motives of gratitude, by rendering these his humble labours useful for promoting the glory of God, as well as profitable and acceptable to his "dear readers"—objects more precious, the Editor firmly believes, to *his* soul, "than thousands of gold and silver."

EDINBURGH,
April 17, 1823.

CONTENTS.

CHAPTER I.

CHAPTER II.

CHAPTER III.

CHAPTER IV.

CHAPTER IV.

CHAPTER V.

CHAPTER VI.

CHAPTER VII.

CHAPTER VIII.

CHAPTER IX.

CHAPTER X.

CHAPTER XI.

CHAPTER XII.

NARRATIVE.

CHAPTER I.

I WAS born of poor but respectable parents, in the town of Peebles, county of Tweeddale, upon the 3d day of April, 1784. Under their nursing care I remained until I was four years of age, when I was sent to my grandfather in Darnick, from whom I received any little education I ever got. Being then too young for school, my grandmother was very attentive in giving me instruction as I was able to bear it; and before I was five years of age, when I was sent to school, I could repeat various psalms, hymns, and passages of Scripture. She employed herself frequently in spinning on the lint wheel, at which time I used to sit at her side, learning verses which she would rehearse to me. I was placed here somewhat like Timothy with his grandmother Lois; for from what I myself recollect, and especially from the testimony of some pious Christians yet living, she was a very eminent character. She laboured much to give me a high veneration for the Supreme Being, in so much that, when I could read a little, I was struck with a kind of reverential dread at the words *Lord* or *God*, when I saw them in the Bible; but I could form no kind of notion what this Great Being could be. As I grew older, my wonder was so far gratified by my worthy instructor telling me that God was a spirit, and invisible, and that I could not speak, act, or even think, but he was acquainted with it all; and that he saw me at all times and in all places: but this I thought could hardly be true, as I imagined God could certainly not see me in the dark.

My grandfather being a very healthy and pious man, no weather would prevent him attending the church at Melrose, which was about a mile distant; but my grandmother being older, and not so robust in her constitution, was often detained at home in stormy weather, or during the winter season; but, though absent in body from the ordinances, she was present in spirit; and it is to be desired that all Christians would improve their time when necessarily detained at home from church as she did; for it was her custom to make family worship, I only being present, during the time of divine service; and it was the greatest possible wonder to me what pleasure she could have in it when my grandfather was absent, and I could take no active part in it, except making an attempt to follow the psalm as she was singing it. It was certainly however a great pleasure to her, though a real weariness to me; but although I could not then see what advantage I could receive from her praying to God to make me an object of his special care, she saw it; and I trust I have reaped much benefit from her prayers. Nor did she lose all the minister's labours, for there were two or three pious neighbours who used to meet upon the Sabbath evening, and talk over the substance of what they had heard, their "speech being with grace, seasoned with salt." My grandfather being a man of superior mental endowments, and having an excellent memory, I was quite astonished how they, and especially he, could remember so much, when, with all my attention, I could scarcely bring home one sentence of what had been preached. I was, however, very careful to learn my task, which was a psalm, or a part of one, and a few questions out of the Assembly's Shorter Catechism; and when I got through that book, I used to answer the whole questions on two Sabbath evenings, to keep them on my memory. In short, I remained under this friendly roof, having the great benefit of precept and example, attending school regularly, until I was eight years of age.

I was then, I may say, sent upon the wide world, in which I have ever since been a wanderer; for, when I came to Edinburgh, where my father and mother then lived, I went to a Mr. ——, in the capacity of a tobacco spinner's boy, where I had of course to mix with many of those I would have chosen to avoid; but, being attentive to my work, my master soon began to take notice of me, and was wont to give me a penny more upon Saturday night than the rest, but this without their knowledge; and his kindness made me if any thing more diligent. I found myself more comfortable here than at first I expected, and I continued in this way until I was ten years of age, when I was hired to a Mrs. C. to wait at the table, run messages, &c. for which I received my meat, clothes, and one pound ten shillings in the half-year.

I was remarkaby well situated in her service, partly through a very trifling circumstance, which was this: When out one day airing, she dropped her gold watch and some money, and I found them and gave them to her in a very cheerful manner, being happy to have it in my power to relieve her uneasy mind; and she took a liking to me, as she said, for my apparent honesty and attention. The first strong proof I had of her attachment was as follows: The housekeeper desired me to bring her a bottle of small beer, and it being somehow not to her mind, she abused me so as to make me cry plentifully; and before I could get myself properly composed, the bell rang, and I was obliged to go up stairs, and, notwithstanding my care not to be discovered, my mistress perceived me in rather a confused state of mind, and asked me the reason in a very kind manner. I was afraid to tell a lie, and her kind treatment emboldened me to acknowledge the truth. After due inquiry, finding the housekeeper in the wrong, and me in the right, she ordered her to get ready to leave the house, but with wages and board wages till the term. Her regard to me still increased, and I did all in my power to please her. In a few weeks after, she sent for my mother, and told her she intended to make a man of me, if we both lived, meaning to give me an education for a genteel business, and to put me in a way to do for myself. My parents were highly gratified with these proposals. But, alas! how uncertain are all human plans and prospects; "For who saith, and it cometh to pass, when the Lord commandeth it not?" The great leveller, who pours contempt upon princes, laid my kind benefactor, "with the hopes of the father that begat me, and of the mother who bare me, low in the dust;" and shall I say, in bitterness of soul, as Jacob did in another case, "that all these things are against me?" Very far be this expression from me; but I have no cause to doubt that, if Mrs. C. had thought herself so near leaving our world, she would have made some provision for me; for the day on which she died, perceiving the approach of the last enemy, she ordered the servant girl who was in the room to ring the bell for me; but her sister-in-law, understanding this, came out of the bed-room, and prevented me entering, saying, I was not wanted, and, as the girl afterwards told me, said to Mrs. C. that I was not in the house. Mrs. C.'s brother-in-law got nearly all her money, houses, and moveables, and only gave me sixpence when I carried his portmanteau to the coach on his leaving Edinburgh. But I was not the only one that sustained a loss by her death; for many poor creatures, who had been her weekly pensioners, mourned their respective losses also. It was really mournful to see these, and her trades-people, and others who had been benefited by her, on the day she was interred, many of them with drooping heads and watery eyes, taking a view of the last remains of their charitable friend; and they had just cause, for even the woman who was her principal weekly pensioner, and had been her nurse, was struck off the list.

My time not being out, I served it out with Mrs. C.'s sister-in-law, and was then engaged with a Mr. B——, who had formerly been in better circumstances, but through some affliction had now lost his sight. My chief business was to go out with him when he wanted an airing; but in this family I experienced a great contrast from that of my valuable friend formerly mentioned, for in truth I was almost starved for want of victuals. It would not become me to tell about the shifts practised in the family, but I remember well being so pinched in my allowance, that I stood eagerly waiting for the potato pot coming off, that I might get the skins to eat, which I would devour with greediness. The servant girl fared no better than myself, and was unable to afford me any relief, as she could not even give me a potato, they being all counted out to her. How much better would it have been for Mr. B——'s two daughters to have done the work of the house themselves, and saved the meat and wages of a servant maid, instead of appearing in public like ladies, when their circumstances were so indifferent! But they had seen better days; "they could not work, and to beg they were ashamed." So true is Solomon's remark, at present as well as in his own day, "There is that maketh himself rich, yet hath nothing."

About this time my worthy grandmother died, (of whom I cannot think without heartfelt emotion,) committing her soul "to Him in whom she believed;" and, as she was exemplary in her life, she was no less so in her death. Although I had not the satisfaction of seeing her on her death-bed, I have since learned some very comfortable particulars. Nothing else worth mentioning happened while I was in this family, but one circumstance; which was this: I happened to get a few halfpence given me, with which I purchased an old fife, and this cheering companion beguiled many a hungry hour, for I was remarkably fond of music. This was not the first time I showed my attachment to music; for when I lived at Darnick with my grandfather, there was a weaver in the town, who was famous, far and near, as a whistler, and he used to gratify my musical desire by whistling a tune to me, till I had got it nearly correct, and then gave me another, and so on; but I was then little aware what this was to lead to, for I afterwards got enough of music, as you shall see in the sequel of this book; but it may be seen from this early propensity in me, that " even a child may be known by his doings."

After leaving this family, I went to a Mr. F. where also was a cousin of my own, who paid me great attention: but I looked upon her rather as an enemy than a friend; for I fell in with some bad companions, with whom I got a habit of staying and amusing myself, when I was sent a message, and in order to screen myself I was obliged to have recourse to falsehoods.—My cousin frequently expostulated with me, but all to no effect; at last my master, discovering my negligent and disobedient conduct, gave me a good drubbing, and this was a mean of bringing me to my senses; so I was compelled to give up all fellowship with my pitch-and-toss gentry, and I became afterwards more attentive. Nothing worth mentioning happened to me while I remained here, but the death of my grandfather, of an iliac passion, who, as I was named after him, distinguished me from the rest by leaving me his Bible as a legacy, wishing the blessing of God to accompany it.

I was now fourteen years of age, and went to learn the trade of a weaver in Darnick; and when you know that the great dearth of 1799, 1800, came on, and that I could only earn about fourteen pence a-day, half of which went to my master, you will see that I had much occasion for the practice of that abstinence which I had been forced to learn at the B— School. It would be tedious and trifling to tell how I managed to make up my breakfast, dinner, and supper; I have been for months together, indeed, that I never could say my hunger was once satisfied, even though I had recourse to rather dishonest means to help me, for I went out at night, and would pull a turnip or two in the fields, when I thought "no eye could see me." But it is worthy of remark, that as far as I can judge, I never knew so much of what contentment was in all my life; I thought hardly any body so well off as myself, for I got into such a rigid system of living, that, through long habit, it became quite natural to me, though I must say that I was often so weak, as hardly to be able to get off and on my loom.

Notwithstanding my very straitened circumstances, I found ways and means, upon the winter Sabbath evenings, to spare a halfpenny for a candle, that I might be able to read Mr. Boston's Fourfold State, to which I had taken a great liking. I delighted particularly to read and meditate on the *Fourth* State, where the happiness of saints in a future world is described; and the expression, "they shall hunger no more," had in it an emphasis (though I fear somewhat of a carnal kind) that put more joy into my heart than worldly men can have when their corn and wine are increased.

During the time I was thus exposed to many hardships, there is one thing I must not omit, which is as follows:—I was rather worse off, both for money and provisions, than I had been for a long time.—No meal was to be had in Darnick, and I went to Melrose on Monday morning for a supply; but the scarcity was so great that I could find none. On Tuesday, after working all the morning, I again went to Melrose, though I was scarcely able to reach it, through weakness, and succeeded in getting a quarter stone at one shilling and fourpence; and all the money I had in the world, after paying this, was twopence. When I was on my way home, walking along the Tweed, I took many a wishful look at my scanty store of meal in the corner of my bag; and taking the twopence out of my pocket, I said to myself, "This is all the money and meal I have to support me till I get my web finished, and the price returned from Edinburgh;" but, to my utter astonishment, I pulled out a shilling along with it. The joy of seeing the shilling, and the unaccountable way of its coming there, filled me alternately with pleasure and pain, but, after recovering from my ecstacy a little, it occurred to my mind, that I must have got it from the miller, through some oversight, in returning me my last twopence in the change for the meal. I resolved, therefore, to go back and return the man his shilling, hungry and weary as I was: but a sinful thought struck me that this might be the hand of Divine Providence, in giving me that mite out of the miller's abundance, to supply my present wants; but I stood and argued with myself long before I could persuade myself to go home and make my supper, of which I stood in much need. In so doing, I acted wrong, and still more so in afterwards thinking that Providence had given a blessing with that shilling, merely because I have never wanted one since—my hardships, I may say, being henceforth at a close.

Shortly after this, the Earlston Volunteers wanted an additional fifer; and as I was still labouring to improve myself, from the time I got the old fife, formerly mentioned, my name reached the ears of the commanding officer, who sent for me, and, with permission of my master, I went every Wednesday afternoon to Earlston, which was about five miles distant, and received each time, one shilling and sixpence for my trouble. My long habit of living meanly, and this addition weekly, made me, as I thought, quite a gentleman, and I saw none that I would have changed conditions with, every thing considered.

After I left Darnick, I went to a Mr. W——, near Dalkeith, and wrought journeyman with him for one summer, during which time, I attended church at Dalkeith ; and I well recollect, that on my way home, having a mile or two of a retired road to go, my mind would frequently be so full of the minister's sermon, and such like topics, that I used to take off my hat and walk bareheaded, as I thought the seriousness of the subject called for that mark of respect, especially as my meditations were mixed with ejaculatory prayer.

I left Mr. W—— after the bleaching work was over for the summer, and went in search of work to Peebles, which, being the place of my nativity, I had a great desire to see. This was, I think, in the year 1802. On my arrival at Peebles I was very fortunate, or rather the Lord made my way prosperous, for I got a good master and comfortable lodgings the very first day. My master was serjeant-major of the volunteers, and being much pleased with my fife playing, he persuaded me to join that corps as a fifer. But soon after the Army of Reserve was raised, and I was obliged, either to pay money into societies, to insure me against it, or run the risk of going for nothing, neither of which I liked. The bounties given to substitutes were very good, and, my excessive regard for music still increasing, I resolved on taking the bounty; but then what excuse to give to my parents I did not well know, for I thought it would vex them much, as I had a brother already in the artillery: so I resolved to say that it was the expense necessary for insuring me, that forced me to go into the army; but in truth it was neither that, nor yet the temptation of the large bounty that made me enlist, but the prospect of being a fifer in the army, where I could get proper instructions in my favourite music. Having made up my mind to this, I offered myself as a substitute for a Mr. G. and received as bounty two and twenty pounds. The report that I had enlisted in the Army of Reserve quickly went over the town, though few believed it, as I was always so attentive to my work, and I had just finished forty-five yards of linen for shirts to myself; but although the news seemed strange to many, it was no more strange than true. So I gave all my best clothes and the web, except as much as made me three shirts, to my mother; and as I did not go to the army from necessity, but choice, I left the whole of my bounty in the hands of a respectable man in Peebles. Along with other recruits, I was marched to Edinburgh, and from thence to Linlithgow, at which place inquiry was made if there was any lad in our party who could play the fife; and the fife-major hearing of me, he asked if I was willing to play on that instrument? I said I had no objection, (for it was indeed the very thing I wanted, as you will easily believe,) provided I was exempted from that disagreeable part of their duty, viz. flogging the men ; so he went to the commanding officer, and got that matter settled to my satisfaction. Shortly after this we received a route for Ireland, and marched on the 5th December. We had snow, rain, or hail every day of our march, which was a fortnight ; but this did not discourage me, for such hardships I had expected, and laid my account with in my new way of life.

CHAPTER II.

We arrived at Belfast, and lay there about six months, nothing extraordinary taking place; only I was truly happy and thankful in having been excused from the disagreeable duty of punishing the men. The very sight of this, for some time, made me ready to faint, until its frequency rendered it easier to my mind. From Belfast we were marched to Athlone, the centre of Ireland, by severe marches. This was in June, 1804. At this place I was appointed leading fifer to the grenadier company of the regiment. We had not been six weeks at Athlone, when an order was issued for forming an army on the plains of Kildare, and our regiment, (the 26th, or Scots Cameronians,) was among the number that assembled at the formation of this camp. When all collected, there were three regiments of horse, sixteen of foot, and a brigade of light infantry, the whole under the command of Lord Cathcart. Here, truly, I began to *peel my wands*, or, to speak more plainly, to know something of the inconveniencies of a soldier's life.

The country being in a very troubled state, we were ordered to encamp on the Curragh, to be ready if wanted, and also to inure us to the hardships of the field. As I said before, I belonged to the grenadiers, and there were twenty of us in a small bell tent; and you may easier conceive than I can describe how such a number could take repose during the night on so small a space, with nothing but straw on the ground, and our camp blankets. We were so jammed together that it was impossible for any one to change his posture, at least without disturbing the whole tent. Our field-days also were very frequent and severe, the men being out from five or six o'clock in the morning until four or five in the afternoon, without tasting a morsel of victuals, so that many of the men fainted daily in the ranks from want and fatigue.

After remaining on the Curragh for six weeks, the country became quiet, and we were ordered back to our old stations; and heartily glad we were again to see the barracks of Athlone. After doing the duty here a few months longer, we received a route to Dublin, at which news I was very greatly delighted, for there I expected to get my musical mind much better entertained than at Athlone. On my arrival at Dublin I went to a music teacher, to whom I paid half-a-guinea a month for getting instructions on the violin and clarionet; but having already acquired considerable execution on the German flute, I was encouraged myself to give instructions on that instrument; and the money I received in this way enabled me to defray the expense of my own teacher, and of buying instruments, music, &c. Here I breathed my native air, I may say; for what with regimental practice, teaching my pupils, attending my own instructions, writing my own music, &c. I certainly had enough of it, yet hardly could I ever say I was satiated. Even in the night the music was passing before me in review; and when I did not perfectly comprehend my master's lessons during the day, they were sure to be cleared up to me when I awoke during the night. There was no time here allowed for the service of God; no—something of more importance, as I thought, engrossed my mind, but I little thought that this course was preparing me apace for falling a victim before a temptation which was not far distant. It may seem strange to my readers, that I who seemed to show so much piety, during my apprenticeship, and for some time afterwards, should now live so careless a life; but I had my lashes of conscience sometimes, I assure you, and endeavoured to hush its clamours by saying, I had no opportunity in a barrack-room for prayer, reading my Bible, or serious reflection, and I tried to believe that God would take this for an excuse, particularly as I promised to become a good Christian, when the Lord should deliver me from this confusion. Truly, the heart is deceitful and desperately wicked. The truth is, my mind was constantly going after its vanities; I found pleasure in nothing but music and musicians.

Windham's plan, as it was called, now came into action. This was for Militia and Army of Reserve men, to volunteer into the line for seven years, and great numbers in our regiment were taking the bounty every day. There was nothing but drumming and fifeing to be heard in the very passages of the barracks, and our commanding officer gave five pounds to drink, night after night, at the mess-house, in order to encourage our men to extend* their service, and enter into the first battalion of the regiment, which consisted of what are called regulars; and to add to the intoxicating effect of the liquor, the whole corps of fifes and drums were ordered to attend, and continued there nightly, till we were all worn out with fatigue. In spite of these temptations, I never once thought of volunteering, though the commanding officer laboured hard to induce me to go with him into the first battalion. I told him freely that my mind did not lead me to the army; and when he saw he could not prevail, he said, "Very well, my man, if your heart does not lie in the right bit, never volunteer." But, alas! the value of the Apostle's admonition, "Let him that standeth take heed lest he fall," was soon after exemplified in my experience. Shortly after this, upwards of one hundred of our men volun-

* The Reserve were enlisted for five years, or during the war, and were not obliged to go out of the three kingdoms.

teered into the 2d battalion of the Scots Royals, which was also a marching regiment. Some of them were asked by Lieutenant-Colonel Stewart if there was any young man of the 26th corps of fifes, that was qualified for fife-major. They all answered, there was one B——. The Colonel hearing so much of me, sent a serjeant to request me to call upon him. This I promised to do next day, but I had truly a miserable conflict in my mind that night, considering whether I ought to accept or refuse this offer. Sleep I could get none, but walked about the passages of the barracks all night, looking anxiously at both sides of the question. My principal objection was the wickedness of the army, for I easily got over that of the hardships to which I would be exposed in a marching regiment, either in the field or in a foreign country. On the other hand, if I could obtain the situation of serjeant and fife-major, the pay would be very comfortable, and I would have an opportunity of seeing the world, which would gratify an inclination I had long entertained. I therefore came to the resolution of going, if I received the above situation. To be short, I went to Colonel Stewart, and after a few words passing on both sides, he asked me if I would take the ten guineas of bounty, and fife-major, with the *rank* of serjeant, and go with him into the 2d Battalion of the Royals. I told him, if I received the *pay*, with the rank of serjeant and fife-major, I would, but not otherwise, for that I did not care for the rank without the pay.— So he was honest enough to tell me, that he did not know if the Duke of Kent would allow a fife-major the pay of serjeant, besides his perquisites as fife-major, but if I would take his offer, he would give me five guineas over and above my bounty, as he had received a good character of me, and liked my appearance, and, moreover, that I would find a friend in him, and that he would write the Duke of Kent, who was our Colonel, for authority to give me the serjeant's pay; but as he could not assure me of its being done, he would promise nothing but what he could perform. This was very honest plain dealing, and was truly attractive in my eyes, but it would not do: so I thanked him for his friendly offers, and so bade him farewell, and walked away; but he followed me to the foot of the stair, where the major of the regiment meeting us, said, "Well Stewart, have you agreed with this young man?" He answered in the negative, and stated to him the reason as above mentioned; but the major soon removed that obstacle, by saying, "we can easily give him the difference of pay out of the fund of the regiment, if the duke will not allow it; and to give me all satisfaction that the serjeant's pay would be sure to me from that date, he offered me his letter to that effect." To this proposal I could no longer object, and in short I received the letter, passed the Doctor, got my bounty, and a furlough of two months to see my friends in Scotland, before I returned to my barracks. A few days after, along with other volunteers, who had also obtained furloughs, we sailed in a vessel for Saltcoats, and, after a very pleasant passage of two days, were safely landed there, and my comrades each took his own road. One young lad only went with me to Edinburgh; and we were on the top of the coach on the 7th day of August, 1806; that dreadful day of thunder, lightning, and rain, by which so much mischief was done to men, beasts, and the fruits of the earth. We were the only outside passengers, and the company inside were willing to incommode themselves considerably, to give us shelter, which was kind on their part, and tempting upon ours; and my comrade gave me the motion to that effect; but I refused, saying, that as we had joined a marching regiment of the line, we must lay our account with being exposed frequently to such weather and worse, and that I could not brook this sort of effeminateness, but no doubt we got a very complete ducking.

I arrived safe at Peebles amongst my old friends, where I was warmly received after an absence of three years; but I did not long remain there till I formed an intimacy with a young woman; and our courtship, like that of many soldiers, was not long; but I would not marry till I returned to the regiment and obtained my Colonel's liberty, that so I might have a better chance of getting her abroad with me, should the regiment, as we expected, be ordered on foreign service. My attachment to this young woman was very sincere; and I gave instructions to the person with whom I had left my bounty money, as formerly mentioned, to give her ten pounds to bear her expenses to the regiment, then in England, when, after obtaining the Colonel's leave to marry her, I should send him a letter to that effect. All being thus settled between us, the time drew nigh when I was to leave my native spot, which was now doubly dear to me. I left Peebles about two o'clock in the morning, in fine moonlight, in the month of September; but it is easier for you, my dear reader, to conceive than for me to describe my situation. I cast many a longing lingering look behind me, and dragged myself by main force out of the view. I was little short of being angry at my preciseness, that I did not marry off hand, and bring the girl with me, whose situation was still more pitiable than my own. We were only two days in Edinburgh, then sailed from Leith Roads for the regiment, which was lying at Horsham, and I was not long there when I had all settled in our favour, and immediately wrote for the young woman; but, as I afterwards discovered, or at least had great reason to suspect, a certain evil-designing person kept up the letters. I waited in anxious suspense for "the girl I left behind me," but I waited in vain. Days were as months, and brought me no relief. At last, to crown my misery, I received a letter from a friend in Peebles, who knew of our agreement, stating, that Jean had almost gone out of her mind about me, and thinking, like too many of my coat, that I was going to prove unfaithful, she went to Edinburgh to inquire about me. There she got no relief to her distracted mind, but only the satisfaction that I had sailed for the regiment at such and such a time. She was now put to her wits end, and in a kind of derangement she wandered to Dumfries, where she had a brother residing, and remained with him for some time. She saw herself like a castaway, for she was ashamed to go back to her place at Peebles, and it being between terms, she could not get into service in a country where she was a stranger: so, in a word, the serjeant of a Highland regiment, an acquaintance of her brother's, paid his addresses to her, and she married him; but scarcely was the festival over when the contents of my letter, through the same channel probably by which it was intercepted originally, reached her ears; and if she was to be pitied before that time, she was not less so then. This was, I may say, my first courtship, (and I then thought it would be my last,) for, during the three years I was in Ireland, I never spent an hour in a woman's company, good or bad, although some of my companions often tried to lead me astray. But I was always so much taken up with my music, that I had no time to spend in such courses: Providence by this means preserving me from at least a worse evil; for these strange women (as Solomon calls them) were the occasion of hundreds of the regiment getting themselves confined and flogged, besides the other dreadful effects produced by their company.

Nothing extraordinary happened till we came to Hastings, which we left on the 15th March, 1807, (on our route to Portsmouth to be embarked for India,) and reached Lewes on that day, where I, and thirty others of our regiment, were billetted at the White

Hart. Shoreham is the next stage for soldiers, and here, intending to write my friends in Scotland, I felt for my watch, (which cast up the day of the month,) that I might put the right date to my letter, but, to my great mortification, my watch was gone. After a little reflection, I remembered that I had, very stupidly indeed, left it in my quarters at Lewes: so I immediately went to Colonel Stewart to ask his permission to return there, which he readily granted. I left Shoreham about four o'clock at night, and reached the inn at Lewes about eleven. Happy was I to find my watch safe in the possession of Boots, and I immediately took the road again, and was in Shoreham in good time to march with the regiment in the morning. When Colonel Stewart saw me, he inquired why I had not gone for my watch; and when I told him I had already been at Lewes, he would scarcely believe me, until I showed her to him. He then desired me to get on one of the baggage waggons; but I said I was able enough for the march; but you may believe I was terribly tired before we reached the next stage.

When we arrived at Portsmouth, the Duke of Kent came in person to make arrangements for the embarkation of the regiment; but now came the tug of war for the married people. There were between two and three hundred women in the 2d Battalion of the Royals, and there were only six women for every hundred men permitted to go; so that sixty women (our battalion being 1000 strong) were the whole number who could embark with their husbands. The selection of these was made by casting lots. Amongst the married people, all was suspense and anxiety to know their destiny; and you may conceive what barrack-rooms we had after it was over. I went into one of them, as I was passing to the Colonel's quarters, to see one of my musical friends, who had a worthy woman to his wife, and to inquire if she had got a prize, but all was *dool* and sorrow. I thought with myself that I would try what my interest with the Colonel could do for this sorrowful couple, but durst not speak my mind lest I should raise hopes that would never be realized, and thus make things worse; for "hope deferred maketh the heart sick." So I opened my mind freely to the Colonel, and spoke much in favour of Mrs. Allan, (for that was her name,) but nothing more than she justly deserved. His answer to me was, "Indeed B—— I wish the Duke of Kent had stopped where he was. We would have managed matters better without him; but I will try what I can do for her on your account. Tell Mrs. Allan to come to me." So I left him quite overjoyed that I should have it in my power to bring comfort to the disconsolate mourners. I returned to his quarters immediately along with Mrs. Allan. The Colonel said, smiling, "Well, Mrs. Allan, are you not afraid of your husband being jealous of you and the Fife Major?" She answered in the negative. "He speaks in very high terms of your character." "I am very much obliged to him, Sir, for his good opinion." "Is he any relation to you?" "No, Sir, but he has always been a very good friend." "That is right; give my compliments to Captain Glover, and desire him from me to put down your name to go with his company."—Take notice of this circumstance, for I will have occasion to mention it again.

CHAPTER III.

We were embarked on board of our respective ships on the 13th April, 1807, and weighed anchor on the 18th. There seems much to make one unhappy and melancholy, when taking probably the last view of the land which gave him birth; but, notwithstanding, all seemed now festivity and joy. Some of those who seemed so full of joy, I have good reason to believe, might, with justice, be called Solomon's merry men—in their laughter their hearts were sad. Still more, perhaps, have their relations who loved them cause of sorrow. To them may the prophet's language be truly directed, "Weep not for the dead, neither bemoan him, but weep sore for him that goeth away, for he shall return no more, nor see his native country; but he shall die in the place where they have led him captive, and shall see this land no more."

At sea, Ship Coutts, May 1*st.* William Troop departed this life. He was one of those unhappy creatures who left his wife behind, and died of a broken heart. They had been lately married, and were like the "loving hind and the pleasant roe," and his feelings being unable to stand the separating stroke, he sunk under this insurmountable load of sorrow.

May 6, Twelve o'clock noon. We had a tremendous storm of wind, accompanied with incessant falls of rain and vivid flashes of lightning. All hands during night were piped by the boatswain upon deck, to reef, or rather to clue the sails, when a fine looking young man, who had shipped himself at Portsmouth for ship's painter, being ordered aloft by the boatswain, to bear a hand in reefing the mizzen topsail, fell from the yard into the sea and was drowned. He pled hard with the boatswain to allow him to remain and assist upon deck, saying, that he never was aloft in his life, and that in such a dreadful night he was sure he would not be able to keep his feet; but all his entreaties were in vain.

June 12. This day we crossed the equinoctial line. The foolish but amusing ceremony (to bystanders) of shaving took place on all those who had not before crossed it; but, lest it might lead to any disturbance, the soldiers were exempted. The form is as follows: A person goes to the head of the ship, in the garb of Neptune, the god of the sea, according to the heathens, and another person, generally the most dexterous at the harpoon, kills a fish previously to this, and gives it to the Captain to be in readiness. Neptune, from the bow of the vessel, hails it in these words, "*What ship, a hoy?*" The officer whose turn it is to be on watch, answers "Coutts," or whatever is the name. "Where bound?" *Officer on watch.*—"India." Neptune then comes on board and enters his triumphal car, which stands in waiting. He is drawn aft by the sailors, and the fish is presented to him by the captain. Then commences the shaving operation. All the sailors who have not formerly crossed the equinoctial are kept below blindfolded until the large tub is ready. Each of them is in this state led upon deck, and placed on a plank laid across the tub, filled with salt water. The mock barber daubs his face all over with tar and feathers.

For a razor he takes a piece of iron hoop and commences his shaving. It requires no common degree of patience to endure this horrid operation; but if the person gets refractory, he is instantly plunged over head and ears in the watery element, by one of the sailors pulling the plank from under him; and after he has scrambled out of the tub, should he stand to expostulate with his comrades on this treatment, two or three of the sailors, each provided with a bucket of salt water, standing on the hammock railings, discharge the contents upon him with such an overwhelming dash as makes him glad to choose another time and place to avenge his wrongs.

June 20. I lost my watch overboard, which cost me upwards of four pounds, and so much uneasiness and travel in England; but I would not have mentioned the circumstance but for the loss of a seal attached to it, which I had received from my affectionate comrade the drum-major of the 2d battalion, who was sent to another battalion, and we got in his place an old wicked creature, whom I may have occasion to bring on the carpet again. We were much attached to each other, and he offered to his Royal Highness to go with me to India in the capacity of a private drummer, if he would not continue him in his present situation; but his petition was not granted, so he gave me this seal as a token of his remembrance.

June 22.—We have seen a great many flying fish lately. This is truly a wonderful curiosity in nature, and is well calculated to excite our admiration and sympathy. These poor persecuted creatures are about the size of a herring, with finny wings, (as they may be called,) resembling in size and shape the blade of a table knife. When pursued by the dolphin, they rise out of the water by the assistance of these wings, and are able to fly as long as they keep moist; they then dip and rise again, until they are quite exhausted, and if they do not gain upon the dolphin, which is not easy, on account of his amazing swiftness in swimming, they become his prey. When out of the water, they seem to be deprived of the use of their eyes, which I suppose was the cause of some of them flying on board of our ship. I one day picked up one, and roasted it upon the gelly fire, and found it to have very much the flavour of a good herring. They always go in shoals; and it is really very novel and beautiful, to see scores, or I may say hundreds of these winged tenants of the great deep, skimming the water like so many swallows.

June 30. James Moor fell overboard when in the act of shaking a rug for one of the officers. He kept himself above water a considerable time, but before the boat which was lowered for his assistance could reach him, he sunk like lead in the mighty waters. The sea was running so high that it was with no small difficulty the boat and crew could reach the ship again.

July 17. We saw the Cape of Good Hope on our larboard bow, but we were at too great a distance to distinguish any objects on land. Signals were hoisted by the ———, 50 gun ship, for the captains, or rather pursers, to give an account of the state of their respective ships with regard to water. Being in general pretty well supplied, except the Coutts, which was head quarter ship, and had upwards of five hundred men on board, the commander of the man-of-war would not put into the Cape for her sake alone. Our expectations of seeing this country were therefore disappointed; but that was nothing: dearly did we pay for the want of this great blessing, with which we could here have been supplied. In about a month after we were put on short allowance, which in these latitudes is an English quart a-day; this we thought very hard, and it was so in some respects; but it would have been well if this allowance had been continued, but from a quart we were speedily reduced to a pint; and in this parched condition were we kept till we reached the land, which was three weeks.

The reader may be inclined to think that this was no great hardship; but I hope you will not take it amiss, if I say that this shows your entire ignorance of the matter. Only consider for a moment, and you will, I am persuaded, come to a very different conclusion. Take for your dinner a salt herring, or a piece of beef that has been perhaps a twelvemonth in the brine, in a very hot summer day, having ate no breakfast beforehand, and try if you would find an English pint of water sufficient even for the afternoon; but what is a single day when the body is full of moisture? Continue this experiment for three weeks or a month, and I am fully satisfied you will change your tone.—Let me tell you, my dear reader, that I never knew the meaning of that passage of the Psalmist, "Let my tongue cleave to the roof of my mouth," before that time; but after lying in my hammock, in the hallop deck, a few hours, (sleeping it could never be called,) amongst two hundred men and upwards, without, I may say, one breath of air, and when the heat was such as to melt the sealing wax I had in my chest—I say, after a person had remained in that state, and in such a place for a few hours, it was hardly possible to articulate a word. You will allow we must have been ill indeed before we could have chosen to be without any victuals cooked for us an entire fortnight. But this was literally the case in the mess to which I belonged. Some of these miserable creatures were so carried away by their intolerable thirst, as to draw up the salt water, in a tin pot, each anxiously waiting his turn to swallow the nauseous draught. This to be sure was making things worse. The consequence of all this was, we had at one time one hundred and thirty-two men on the doctor's list, with sea-scurvy and sores. You will think it strange that we could live at all after so long wanting victuals. I answer, we had a certain quantity of biscuit served out to us, all the colours of the rainbow; and I am sure the pint of water, which we had every day at twelve o'clock, would, from taste and smell, have turned the stomach of any person who had never known any thing of this extremity. A person possessed of the best eyes in the ship could not see to the bottom of a tea-cup full of it, had he got it to himself for his trouble, which would have been the greatest reward that could have been offered to him. You may think I am going to say too much, but I say it with a clear conscience, that in this state of torment I would have cheerfully suffered the *pain* of drowning, (but not to be drowned outright, mind ye,) for a bellyful of water; and often, in my troubled slumbers, did I imagine myself plunging and struggling in the waters of the Tweed, and I "dreamed, that behold I was drinking, but when I awoke, behold I was faint, and my soul had appetite." My dear reader, I pray to God that you may never experience this extremity, for the pain of hunger, which I have often felt, was pleasure itself compared with these sufferings.

CHAPTER IV.

DURING this voyage, which was five months to a day, we observed land twice at a great distance, viz. the Cape of Good Hope, and the Island of Sumatra: we had six men died, and two fell over board. But the land which we so eagerly desired appeared upon our starboard bow upon the 13th of September, 1807. This island was formerly called Punang, but the modern name is, Prince of Wales' Island, and is situated at the straights of Malacca. The land has a very fine appearance when tolerably near, having a gentle declivity toward the sea, and mantled over with wood. But it was the water which we longed for, and the hope of which raised our spirits more than the view of the truly welcome scenery which we were approaching.

We remained on board of our respective ships until the 18th, when all were ordered ashore; the sick men (at least those who were very bad) to the general hospital, and the effective to the barracks. But we sent more men to the general hospital than all the rest of the fleet, which proves the bad consequences produced by scarcity of water; for all the rest of the ships had three times our quantity, exclusive of their having pease soup twice a week, which we were deprived of, from the want of water. We had to march about three miles before we came to the barracks, at the back of which there was a small rivulet; and you may easily suppose that we were no sooner dismissed from the ranks, than it was who to be first there, to enjoy once more the unspeakable luxury of fresh water. But this had none of the best effects, for the water being impregnated with the juice of the different kinds of sweet fruits that fell from the trees of the plantation through which it flowed, and our long abstinence, contributed not a little to bring on a severe flux, which cut off the men in great numbers. Our accommodation here was indeed very indifferent, and not at all what we expected from the idea of India which we had formed to ourselves, from what we were accustomed to hear when at home.

The barracks were very temporary, being entirely made from the cocoa-nut tree, and were divided into five rooms, or rather houses, clear from end to end, and containing each about one hundred and eighty men. The walls, or rather sides of these houses, were made by stakes driven into the ground, and were about nine feet high, and these stakes covered over with cocoa-nut leaves, spitted like candlewicks, and tied in horizontal rows, one over another from top to bottom. The roof was formed nearly as it is in this country, and covered with the same materials as the sides. And when it came to blow hard, which it frequently did, and these leaves gave way to the blast, the barracks had the appearance of waving corn in harvest. Our beds also were as temporary as our barracks, being also stakes driven into the ground, and spaked over from end to end like a horse's hack for holding hay, without any bedding whatever, even for the sick in the regimental hospital! It was therefore a happy thing for the men that brought their hammock and blanket ashore, for those who sold them to the bum-boats (that came along-side with fruit) were obliged to lie with their body clothes, upon these knotty bamboo spakes, which made them any thing but a comfortable place for repose.

We knew a great difference also of our provisions from what we had been accustomed to at home; for we were served out with buffalo beef, on which there was not to be seen a shred of fat; and rice was our substitute for bread. This was very well for the natives, who knew nothing else; but for men accustomed to the rich and substantial food of Europe, and particularly after the stomach had lost all relish by a wasting dysentery, it was very sorry fare, and made us incline to adopt the sentiments of the Israelites, and to long for the flesh pots of that land we had left.

We were a very few days here when the flux appeared amongst the men, and made very rapid progress. I also took this trouble, which increased upon me to a very great degree. I acknowledge myself to have acted a very imprudent part, in not reporting myself to the doctor sooner; but I was at last compelled to put my name into the sick list, when I was well told of my error; and as I was found to be in a dangerous condition, I was sent to the general hospital, where all the worst of our men were; for the medical officers there were better acquainted with the nature of this disease, and the accommodation was also much better for the men. The manner in which the sick are conveyed in this country, is as follows :—The person is put into what is called a doolie, which is nearly in the form of one of the small houses or boxes used in Scotland for watch-dogs, being about six feet long, and three deep. In the middle of each side there is a door to go out and in by, and upon the top, at each end, there is a strong ring, through which a pole is put, and borne by four natives. I was therefore laid in one of these doolies, and carried about half way, when the bearers stopt. I conjectured that they were resting a little, as it was three miles between the barrack and the hospital; but I was rather surprised when one of them demanded some money from me. I told him that I had nothing for him; but that I would give him something when they carried me to the hospital. This did not at all satisfy him; and the other bearers also became clamorous, and I began to fear they intended me a mischief,—for they might have done what they chose with me, as I was unable to make any resistance, being both feeble and unarmed; but I got them to proceed, by giving signs to them that they should be rewarded for their trouble afterward. But I never heard a word about money when they set me down; and if I had reported them to the general doctor, they would have been paid for their trouble with a witness: but as they made off when I left the doolie, I said nothing about it.

When I entered the hospital, and looked around me to view the place, and saw the meagre and distressed features of the men stretched upon the beds, and many of the cots empty, as if death had been robbing the place of its inhabitants, to replenish the narrow house appointed for all living, something awfully solemn stole upon my mind, which I could by no means shake off, and which I am altogether unable to describe. I had not remained here many days when I thought my disorder was taking a turn for the better; but I was deceived in this, because it was only some temporary relief I was receiving from the medicine, for it returned upon me worse than ever. Here I had wearisome nights appointed to me, for in that season I was generally worst. The ward in which I lay was very large, and had a truly dismal appearance at night, being lighted by two or three glimmering lamps, while all around was solemn and still, save the cries and groans of the sufferers, that seemed to contend along the echoing walls; and night after night we were visited by the king of terrors, to many, I am afraid, in his awfulest form. There were no less than six of his darts struck the next cot to that on which I lay.

You may think that my state in these circumstances was truly deplorable, and you think rightly, for so it was; but I have not told you the worst, for "the spirit of a man may sustain his infirmity," and my spirit was not easily subdued by affliction, but "a wounded spirit who can bear?" and "The arrows of the Almighty were within me, the poison whereof drunk up my spirits," for here I had time for serious reflection, or rather here it was forced upon me. Here I could not mix with jolly companions to drive away melancholy, and my favourite music could give me no relief. Here too I was compelled to listen to the voice of conscience, and O! how loudly did it expostulate with me about the answers I formerly gave it in Ireland, namely, that I had no opportunity in the confusion of a barrack-room for reading my Bible, meditation, or prayer, but that I would become a good Christian when I was out of the army. Here I was indeed out of the confusion of a barrack-room, but not only still in the army, but far, far from any minister of Christ to give me wholesome counsel. O what would I have given for the company of a godly minister, or pious, well-informed Christian! but, alas! "I looked upon the right hand, but none would know me; refuge failed me, no man cared for my soul."

Surely the Lord frequently answers the prayers of his people by "terrible things in righteousness." Here, "in the multitude of my thoughts within me," I could entertain little hope of ever coming out of this place again, far less of getting out of the army, where I might have an opportunity of serving God; for death seemed to be making rapid strides towards me, to take me down to the "bars of the pit." But death seemed rather a relief from my agonizing trouble, had it not been that I knew that "after death there was a judgment." And how was my soul to appear before the holy and just Judge of the earth? This was a question I could not answer. I looked with anxious care to see if any hope was to be entertained from my past life, but, alas! all seemed to be a dreary waste. Some comfort, indeed, I had from the view of my apprenticeship, and some time afterward, which I formerly mentioned; but, alas! even then I saw myself to have been guilty of many a sin, and all the rest of my life appeared to be but one act of disobedience and rebellion; and I saw myself condemned by the laws of heaven, supposing I had lived all my life in the apparently innocent manner above stated; for it is written, "Cursed is every one that continueth not in all things which are written in the book of the law, to do them." I next looked to the general mercy of God, but neither could that give me any relief; and in this state of torment I remained for several nights and days with little intermission. At last it pleased the Lord to send me relief in the following manner:—

One forenoon, when I was almost distracted with the agony of my soul, and the pain of my body, that blessed passage was given me, "Call upon me in the day of trouble; I will deliver thee, and thou shalt glorify me:" and never before did I feel any thing come home with such divine power and such healing comfort to my afflicted soul. I tried to recollect if ever

I had read it in my Bible, or heard it any time, but in vain; yet I was fully persuaded that it was the voice of God speaking in his word, and accompanied by his Holy Spirit. I will not attempt a description of my mind at this time, for it is impossible, because it was indeed "a joy unspeakable." O what a flood of comfort did it impart to my helpless soul! for then I believed that God "had not in anger shut up his tender mercy, but still intended to be gracious." Now "the Lord made my bed in my sickness," for my couch, as I thought, became softer, and every thing around me wore a different aspect. I yet looked back with pleasure to the description of heaven given by Mr. Boston in his Fourfold State, (which I used to read when in Darnick,) and still hoped to be an inhabitant of that happy place. Here the Lord turned for me "my mourning into dancing, he put off my sackcloth, and girded me with gladness;"—here the Lord dealt with me as he did with his ancient church, for "he allured me, and brought me into the wilderness, that he might speak comfortably unto me;"—and here "he made me to sing, as in the days of my youth." "Sing unto the Lord, O ye saints of his, and give thanks at the remembrance of his holiness: For his anger endureth but a moment; in his favour is life; weeping may endure for a night, but joy cometh in the morning." My dear reader, if you are a stranger to the comfortable sense of the favour of God, you may think this is strange kind of language; and no wonder, for "the natural man receiveth not the things of the Spirit of God, for they are foolishness unto him: neither can he know them, because they are spiritually discerned;" but believe me, this was true solid comfort, arising from a view which I had just obtained of a reconciled God in Christ, although I acknowledge myself to have had at this time a very imperfect knowledge of the gospel-scheme of salvation.

Yet the Lord, who generally works by rational means, left not his work half done, for he sent me an instructor in the following manner:—The next day there was a young man, who sailed out with me in the same ship, came and sat down upon my bed-side. He had been in the hospital for some time, but I had never seen him, nor even known that he was in the place, because he was in a different ward. I had even a very slight acquaintance of him as a fellow-soldier, and none at all of his being an eminent Christian. As I said, he sat down upon my bed-side, and asked very kindly how I was. My heart warmed to him while he uttered the words, though I cannot tell for what, but I formed somehow a favourable opinion of him, and was free enough to tell him how matters stood. I began by informing him how my mind had been exercised since I came to the hospital, nearly in the way above related, as I wished to hear his mind upon the subject, lest I should be deceiving myself. He asked me, if I read my Bible. I said, that I had sometimes read it when I could see, but could derive very little comfort from it, as I could not understand it; and now my sight was so far gone as to be unable to read it, but I would take it kind if he would read a portion of it for me,—which he readily agreed to. But, oh! the rays of light that darted into my mind while he read, and "opened to me the Scriptures!" I then spoke to him of my former wicked, unprofitable life. He said, "The blood of Jesus Christ, God's Son, cleanseth from all sin." I then said, the only comfort I could derive from the many years I had lived, was when a very young boy, as I have formerly stated; but I saw that although I had lived all my life in this comparatively harmless way I was condemned; for it is written, "Cursed is every one that continueth not in all things written in the book of the law, to do them." He answered, "That whatever the law saith, it saith to them that are under the law, that every mouth may be stopped, and all the world become guilty before God;" but that "Christ Jesus had redeemed us from the curse of the law, by being made a curse for them who walk not after the flesh, but after the Spirit;" and moreover, "it was not by works of righteousness which we have done, but according to his mercy he saved us, by the washing of regeneration, and renewing of the Holy Ghost, shed on us abundantly through Jesus Christ our Saviour." After some conversation of this kind, we took leave of each other, he promising soon to come back and see me. I need hardly tell you how we frequently "took sweet counsel together," while he remained in the hospital; but his complaint getting better, he was ordered to his duty, which truly I was very sorry for. But by God's kindness in sending me this instructor, I was put into the way that leads to everlasting life; and my mind being led into "wisdom's ways, which are pleasantness and peace," my body began gradually to recover.

The flux, however, still continuing, and keeping me in a state of extreme weakness, I was advised by one of my fifers to take a dose of corks and wine without the doctor's knowledge, since all his medicine hitherto appeared ineffectual for stopping the flow of blood. I was rather averse to this prescription, which was a pint of wine, made as warm as I could possibly drink it, and a burnt cork reduced to a powder and mixed with it, and this dose I was to take for three nights; and, to encourage me, he said some of our former regiment were cured by it when we were in Ireland. I accordingly took this horse medicine with great difficulty; and you may easily imagine that it could not be otherwise, considering that I had eaten nothing for about a fortnight; and more particularly, that my mouth was perfectly raw with the mercury which is given in obstinate cases of this disease, and the cork stuck in my throat, so that it was hardly possible for me to get it over; however, I got it managed for the three nights; but never would I advise a friend of mine to try such an experiment, for the pain of the flux was never so severe as that produced by this savage dose. After being a few days in this extreme pain, the flux of blood disappeared, and I got gradually better, but I have never enjoyed my former health; and, I believe, stopping the blood so suddenly was permanently unfavourable to my constitution.

I must not omit informing you, that my good friend the Colonel, with whom I enlisted in Dublin, used to pay me a visit frequently; and finding me in better health and spirits than formerly, he told the doctor to let me want for nothing which could be of service to me. The doctor then inquired very particularly into my case. I told him the blood had left me, and that my mouth was rather better. He ordered me a pint of wine every day, and a bit of fowl for dinner. In a word, by the blessing of God, I got a good deal better, and left the hospital upon the 9th November; but I had not been at my duty many days, when an order came for seven companies to go to Madras, by a frigate and two country ships, which were ready for us in the bay. We embarked upon the 25th November, the staff and light company went on board of La Dedaigneuse, a frigate formerly taken from the French; and the rest of the regiment (except two companies left at the island) went on board of the two country ships. We had a very rough passage, having high winds, swelling seas, and a leaky ship; and being exposed to the weather, as we took our watch upon deck in turns, I was again seized with a severe flux. The Colonel, seeing me one day on deck, inquired very kindly how I was? I told him the truth;

and he was very angry that I should expose myself in such weather, especially after my late severe illness. I made the best apology I could, but he was not satisfied, and desired me to go to the surgeon and let my case be known. He likewise asked me what liquor I received? I told him half a pint of arrack daily; but I said that I did not think that it was agreeing with me. So he spoke to the doctor, who ordered me a pint of wine in place of it, and to keep myself constantly below. The frigate, as I have stated above, was very leaky; and having to encounter a dreadful hurricane during four nights and days, it was with difficulty that the crew, with the assistance of the soldiers, could keep her afloat. We were three weeks upon this passage without any deaths, except one man who fell overboard; but it was indeed a very disagreeable voyage, for we could not keep our provisions from getting wet by the sea rushing in between every plank! You may think it strange that one of his Majesty's ships of war was suffered to be in this leaky condition; but it would have taken a very tight vessel indeed to have ridden this storm without making a considerable quantity of water; and, moreover, she was ordered for dock as soon as she reached the harbour.

The manner of landing persons on this coast may not be unworthy of the reader's attention. The best boats belonging to his Majesty's navy dare not venture through the prodigious surf that runs every where on the beach, and you may often see the captains of the Indiamen or Men-of-war, obliged to leave their elegant boats and fine-dressed crews outside the surf, and get on board of what are called Massulah boats, to be rowed ashore by natives. These boats are constructed nearly like our own, but are considerably deeper. The planks are sewed together by small cocoa-nut ropes, instead of being nailed, and they are caulked by the cocoa-nut hemp (if I may call it so) of which the ropes are made.

When the passengers are all seated, the boatmen begin their rowing, which they accompany with a kind of song, until they approach the breakers, when the boatswain gives the alarm, and all is activity among the rowers; for if they did not pay great attention to avoid the wave in the act of breaking, the boat would run every risk of being swamped. The most severe part of the boat's usage is when she strikes the beach the first time, which generally tumbles the passengers upon one another like a heap. The boatmen must not attempt to jump out and pull her ashore after the first breaker, for the wave that makes her strike runs past a considerable distance, and then returns, rushing down the declivity of the beach with irresistible force, carrying her along with it; but before the next wave overtakes them the boat has gained a little by rowing, so that the second shock is less formidable; and, on the third, they jump out in a moment, and lay hold on a rope fastened to the bow on purpose, and thereby hold her fast till the passengers get ashore. Were our boats to get such usage it would knock them to staves.

After our landing, we were encamped upon the south esplanade, which divides Fort St. George from the original town of Madras.

CHAPTER IV.

I do not here intend to give a particular account of Madras; but as your curiosity may be somewhat excited, I will gratify it a little, by giving you a kind of general description. Madras, or Fort St. George, (sometimes distinguished into Black Town and White Town,) the principal settlement of the British, on the coast of Coromandel, has a very beautiful appearance from the sea; and the first sight of this place is not calculated to spoil the picture which a sanguine imagination draws to itself. The clear, blue, cloudless sky, and the polished white buildings, of which there is a great number, both in the Fort and along the beach, present a combination entirely new to the British traveller, which is well fitted to give him a very exalted idea of India, and lead him to imagine, after being so long out of the sight of land, that he is entering a new world, something far superior to that which he has left. But it is with this as with the work of the painter; for it looks best at a distance. That part of the town which is within the fortress can boast indeed of several fine streets; and the houses being covered with a kind of stucco, called *chunam*, which is capable of a polish little inferior to marble, have a very elegant and lively appearance: but as to the houses of the original town, sometimes called by the natives, Madras *Patnam*, (which signifies *superior*,) no rule seems to have been followed but that of contrast; for the fine white polished buildings of the European, the Persian, or the Indian merchant, are promiscuously interspersed with the most wretched mud-walled cocoa-nut covered huts of the poorest native: and the confused, irregular, unpaved streets, render it one of the dirtiest places possible in wet weather. There are a number of meeting-houses here for the various religious professors; but that which has the most respectable appearance, (the protestant church of Fort St. George excepted,) belongs to the Armenians. The appearances of the natives also are extremely varied; and we find it hold good here, as in other parts of the world, "that the poor and the rich meet together;" for we here see some carried in palanquins shoulder high, and others performing all the offices of drudgery; while some are riding in their bullock coaches, others are walking on foot, following their various employments; while some are riding upon horses, well clothed, with ear-rings the circumference of a large tea-cup, others are hardly able to walk, but literally, "wretched, and miserable, and poor, and blind, and naked." That feature in the female character which has been general in all ages, is also very prominent in this place: for we find many of the wealthy of that sex adorned with all the varieties of toys mentioned by the prophet, "walking with stretched forth necks, and wanton eyes; walking and mincing as they go, and making a tinkling with their feet;" but it is the less to be wondered at, that these poor creatures should take such a pride in showing themselves off, as they think, with these butterfly ornaments; for they know no better: but it is truly a pity, as well as a great sin, that the daughters of Zion in our own land should so far follow their example, and expose themselves to the judgments of the Lord for the sake of a few trinkets, as those women did in the days of the prophet. Because it is very evident, that it was the sin which these daughters of Zion contracted, by setting their affections upon these vanities of ornaments, that was the cause of God denouncing his judgments against them. It would surely be infinitely better, to adorn themselves according to the direction of the apostle; "whose adorning," said he, "let it not be that outward adorning of plaiting the hair, and wearing of gold, or putting on of apparel; but let it be the hidden man of the heart, in that which is not corruptible, even the ornament of a meek and quiet spirit, which is, in the sight of God, of great price."

While our regiment lay at Madras, we were infested by the natives offering themselves for servants, and many of them did get into place; but, I believe those that took them would have been much better without servants, for they plundered them of what they could get, and then went their way*.

* Most of these fellows belonged to the thieving bazaar, (a market here for receiving and selling stolen goods,) and took this method of obtaining some booty. I think it is a great shame (to say no worse of it) that such a place should be protected by law; for the goods taken from us could not be gotten from thence unless they were regularly paid for, in the same manner as

We lay in camp upon the south esplanade until the 20th, when we got the route for Wallajahbad. This being our first march in the country, we had our provisions and baggage carried free, but very few of us thought much of the meat, and less of the liquor; for the arrack used to be standing all night in cocoa-nut shells, and spilled upon the ground in the morning when we marched. It would have been well for the far greater part of our regiment, had this indifference to that liquor continued; but, alas! it was far otherwise, as I yet may have cause to observe.

We came to Wallajahbad upon the 24th December, 1807. This place was to us ac-

if we had never seen them; but if the thief was caught before he reached the bounds assigned for the bazaar, he could be prosecuted and punished. As a proof of what I have stated, Captain M'Lean of our regiment had his regimental coat stolen, and it was found there, but he durst not touch it without agreeing with the bazaar man for a certain sum. However, before I left the country, they were much restricted, no goods being allowed to be publicly exposed until four o'clock in the afternoon.

cording to its name, for it proved very *bad* to our regiment; the men, women, and children, dying almost every day. As fife-major of the regiment, it was part of my duty to warn a fifer for the funeral party always upon evening parade, for the following day; and there were twelve days successively that the fifer for the funeral was wanted. Although there were none dead at the time, I ordered him to be in readiness; and for that space of time, we never missed one day without having less or more paying the debt of nature. If a man died at night, he was buried in the morning; and if through the day, he was interred in the evening. Amongst the many that died at this time, my old musical friend Allan was one. He was cut off by water in the head; but the disorder that carried off almost all the rest was the bloody flux, or dysentery.

About this time the grenadier company (which had parted with us upon our voyage to get their ship refitted) joined us*, and also the two companies from Prince of Wales's Island. The grenadiers were, in

* The grenadiers who were on board of the East India Company's ship, Surat Castle, had been obliged to part with the fleet, in consequence of the leaky state of that vessel, when we were near the latitudes of South America, and with difficulty reached the port of Rio Janeiro. But had it not been for the extraordinary exertions of these able-bodied men, the ship, and every soul on board, must, in all human probability have perished; for they were under the absolute necessity of working the pumps night and day for a considerable time before they reached that port, and, notwithstanding all their endeavours, the water gained upon them to such a degree as to be two or three feet deep upon the harlop deck; but in spite of their excessive hardships and fatigues, that company was the most healthy of any in the regiment. For during the whole voyage they had very little sickness, and none of their numbers diminished by death, in a natural way. They had, indeed, one struck dead by a thunderbolt, and another killed by the natives of a certain island, where they touched for a supply of fresh water. The way that this man came into the power of these savages was as follows:—A party of the grenadiers were sent ashore with a few water casks to get them filled, and while they were performing this piece of duty, some misunderstanding took place between them and the natives; and the soldiers not being aware that they were going to get

general, envied by the rest of the regiment for their healthy appearance; but, alas! that did not long continue; for no less than

such rude treatment, were quite unprepared with weapons offensive or defensive, so that some of them were cut and mangled most dreadfully by their assailants. But the man I allude to, whose name I do not recollect, and another of the name of Campbell, with whom I was very intimate, wrested each a weapon from the blacks, and, as the saying is, "made their own sticks break their own heads;" and, in this manner fought their way, retreating backward toward the boat, which some of their companions had reached; but before they could attain their object, the poor fellow sunk under the repeated blows of his overpowering enemies, and Campbell received seven severe wounds, several of which were in the head. Those who had not the good fortune to reach the boat were taken prisoners. No sooner did the news of this disaster reach the ship than the officers were fired with indignation at the treatment which their men had received, and the soldiers, particularly, for losing several of their comrades, while those who escaped came on board streaming with blood. Such outrages were not to be tamely submitted to by those who had not only the name, but also the courage, of British soldiers. Orders were immediately given for the men to get ready their arms and ammunition, to go in quest of their companions who were detained ashore, and these orders were attended to with all the alertness that could have been displayed had the ship been twenty-one of these robust looking men went the way of all living in the course of one month.

March 3, 1808, I was married to Mrs.

on fire, and they themselves obliged to fly for their lives to a safe and commodious shelter. No sooner were the grenadiers landed than they marched steadily towards a town not far from the shore, where the king lived, defying all opposition to their progress, and striking terror into the hearts of every beholder. And when they reached the place, the determined countenances of the men, and the dazzling appearance of their shining arms, so enervated the hearts and arms of his majesty's loyal subjects, that they could make little resistance until our party was in the royal presence itself. One of the men, named John Love, literally took the poor trembling Nabob by the neck like a dog, and the royal suite, seeing his majesty treated so unceremoniously, perceived well what was to be their fate if they continued to hold the soldiers in their place of confinement, and therefore prudently made all the haste in their power to restore them to the embraces of their brave messmates, who all returned to the ship in safety, and were warmly received by those on board. My wife has now the pillow that the Captain gave to Campbell, to lay under his mangled head, after he went on board. However, with proper medical attendance, and kind treatment, he recovered, and was raised to the rank and pay of serjeant after the company joined in Wallajahbad.

Allan. This is the circumstance I told you to mark before we left England, after I had obtained liberty from Colonel Stewart for her to go with her husband. But I had then very little knowledge that I was taking out a wife for myself, and one too, that was to be the means in the hand of Divine Providence of prolonging my days, for had it not been for her nursing care, I must, in all human probability, have gone the way of hundreds of the regiment, as I had much severe trouble after I was joined to her. She had no children, save one daughter that was left at home with her grandfather, whom I may have occasion to speak of afterwards. I was in a very poor state of health when married to her; for the complaint I caught in the frigate had never left me, and I really had at that time more need of a doctor than a wife; but I knew her to be an excellent woman, and as she had no objections to me as a husband, I could have none against her as a wife; but happily for me I found in her both a doctor and a wife, and I daily recovered and enjoyed a tolerable state of health for some time.

May 22.—The government at Madras being informed by our returns that we were in a very bad state of health, sent an order for us to proceed to Sadras, a seaport, for the benefit of our health. At this time we could not muster five hundred effective men in a regiment upwards of a thousand strong; but we were now doomed to still more lamentable misfortunes, for more than three hundred men fell sick the first day's march; chiefly of brain fevers, attended with a dreadful discharge from the bowels, and twelve men belonging to the regiment died the same day: six of whom marched to the ground with their arms and accoutrements. The heat was intense, with scarcely a breath of air, and any that there was, was as hot as if it had issued from a baker's oven. One of our men who had formerly been in the country fourteen years, with the 74th regiment, said that he never recollected of having suffered so much in one day from heat. Many of the men had recourse to throwing water upon themselves, but they could get no relief from this expedient, because it was quite warm; and what added much to their distress, was the utter want of perspiration. My wife also suffered much from a checked perspiration, and I thought of a method that gave her great relief, which was this; I dipped a hand towel in water, and gave it a slight wring, and stood over her while she lay upon the ground, waving it backward and forward; this, from the quick evaporation, cooled her greatly, and gave her considerable relief. My comrades also, to whom I mentioned it, derived similar benefit from this plan. The men who were very bad, were taken into marquees erected on purpose for them; but this expedient, which gave many who were not very ill considerable relief, was of no use to them. All that the surgeon (for we had only one with us) could do for them, was to let blood at the temples, and having filled two large marquees with those who were worst, the rest had to assist one another in their tents the best way they could; but at last the doctor falling ill himself, had recourse to bleeding his own temples by the assistance of a looking-glass, and lay down amongst the rest of the sick men. Thus, being deprived of all medical assistance, and many of the men running about mad, and others dying in the marquees before the Colonel's eyes; he was so overcome by the sight that he could not refrain from tears. The poor unhappy creatures who were attacked with this temporary derangement, had in general some idea that they were not in their own country. One of these runaways being asked where he was going, said, that he was going to Europe; and added, that if he was once there, he would soon be well again. However, when the cool of the evening arrived, a number of the men got considerably better; about mid-day when the men were in such an alarming state, the Colonel had sent off an express to the commandant of Wallajahbad, describing the melancholy situation of the regiment; and we immediately received medical assistance, and more doolies and waggons to carry the sick, with an order to return to our barracks. This was welcome news for us; and we accordingly returned to Wallajahbad the next day, carrying along with us one hundred and fifty sick men who were unable to march.

September 4.—We had prayers read for the first time since we came to this country, by the adjutant, who had fifty pagodas a-month for doing the duty of chaplain. But this was, I think, little short of making a mock of the divine ordinances; for here was truly, "like people, like priest." Oh for an opportunity of hearing a good sermon, from the mouth of a godly minister of Jesus Christ. "O God, thou art my God; early will I seek thee: my soul thirsteth for thee, my flesh longeth for thee in a dry and thirsty land, where no water is; to see thy power and thy glory, so as I have seen thee in the sanctuary."

November 4.—My good friend Colonel Stewart left us, in consequence of liberty received from the government, to return to his native country for the benefit of his health; as he had long been labouring under a severe liver complaint. I was truly sorry for his departure, as I thought his loss to me could never be repaired; but I was in this happily mistaken; for he recommended me to the particular notice of Colonel Conran, his successor, who treated me constantly with the greatest kindness; although the men generally formed a very bad opinion of him at first, for he used to take out the triangles to evening parade; and if any of the men were unsteady in the ranks, he tried them by a drum-head court martial, and flogged them upon the spot; but this was not because he delighted in punishment, but to make the regiment steady and attentive, which they were not out of the need of. He was, to give him his due, "a terror to evil doers, and a praise to them that do well."

January 13, 1809.—We left Wallajahbad, in consequence of a route to proceed to Bangalore. This was a very melancholy day for many. We could not avoid thinking of the great number of our comrades whom we left behind; having, in little more than one year, formed a grave-yard of about two hundred men, women, and children! but after we had proceeded on our march four days, we were countermanded, and sent again to Madras.

February 3.—We took the duty of the garrison from the 30th regiment, which marched out, and we occupied their barrack. Not long after we came here, I was visited with a severe fever. I now found a kind friend in Colonel Conran; for he paid great attention to me during my illness; sending me fowl, wines, sugar, and even fruits, which he thought would be beneficial in my disorder. He even came in person frequently to see me, and ordered the Doctor to attend me in my own room, which he appointed for me himself; and, by the blessing of God upon the use of means, I recovered in about three weeks. While we lay in Madras, there arose a disturbance among the Company's troops; and it being reported that they intended to attack the fort, the artillery were ordered to provide a sufficient quantity of ammunition for their reception, which was distributed proportionally to each gun; but it was never required, for they were wiser than make such a foolish attempt. The insurrection in the high country, however, getting rather serious, an order was issued for an army to be formed to suppress it. This mutinous spirit was said to have been excited by the Governor taking away the staff situations of a number of the Company's officers, in different forts through the country, making one do the duty of two, and sending the other to his regiment in his former situation. For instance, in many of these forts there were (what is called) a fort-adjutant and a quarter-master of the fort: now, one of these had to do the duty of both, for which he received no more than his former pay. The sepoys (native soldiers) were not in much better humour; for they were dissatisfied because they did not receive the pay of European soldiers, saying, that as they did the same duty, and were exposed to the same hardships, they were entitled to the same allowances. On the other hand, the government stated, that European soldiers had removed from their own country, and should therefore be distinguished from natives of this country, who besides could live much cheaper. However, this statement did not satisfy them; and from less to more, they proceeded so far as to take some of the forts into their own possession, and were headed by Company's officers of the dissatisfied party. Things could not remain long in this state of confusion; and to compel the mutineers to desist from their purpose of destroying all order amongst the forces, an army was formed at three different stations, to proceed to the high country in various directions. Our Colonel being a man of great military skill, was appointed to command the centre division of the army, which was formed at St. Thomas's Mount, seven miles from Madras, upon the 8th day of August, 1809. This division of the army consisted of ten pieces of artillery, two regiments of horse, the Royal Scots, 66th and 89th Europeans, two hundred pioneers, and the 8th and 20th regiments of native infantry.

An order was also issued by our commanding officer for all the heavy baggage, women, and boys, to be left at Madras. This was sorrowful news for the married people, and my wife was much grieved to hear them, particularly as I was then but weakly, and not very able to encounter the hardships to which I would thus be exposed. She was therefore eager to go with the regiment, that she might know the worst of it. I tried all I could to dissuade her from going, but in vain; and, in short, she being a stout healthy woman, and having no children to incommode us, she was permitted to go, to my great benefit, as well as her satisfaction; for truly, had it not been for her, it would have fared but badly with me upon the march, as I will afterwards make appear.

CHAPTER V.

August 27.—We entered the territories of the Poligars. At this pass we were met by three of the Company's revenue collectors flying for shelter to our army, having been robbed of all their wealth by a party of the rebels. We here see the dreadful condition of a country, where all laws, divine and human, are put at defiance. We received a visit from the Nabob of this district of country, who is tributary to our government, accompanied with all his retinue. He himself, and suite, were mounted on elephants, upon the back of which was placed a square tower, covered with crimson velvet; but the greater part of his guards were upon horseback, and those of them who were upon foot carried a kind of pike twelve feet long, which they manage with great dexterity. When they wish to strike an object, they place the one end of the pike upon the right arm, and after giving it a powerful throw, they immediately pull it back by a coil of rope which is held in their left hand, the one end of which rope is of course fastened to the pike. This country is very mountainous, and abounds with tigers and wild boars, (particularly the latter;) but there is a species of dog here that is a mortal enemy to the wild boar; and but for these useful creatures, the natives would often run great dangers from their bold and ferocious attacks. Our officers killed one at this camp-ground, which I saw: it was nearly equal in size to one of our middle-sized hogs, but apparently much more active, with terrible tusks.

September 21.—For this some time past we have been marching through woods, and jungles, and by impassable roads, until our pioneers made them passable, by cutting trees, and covering them with sods, so that there might be a passage for the guns and bandies*; and it was very seldom that we could get any victuals to buy for money; because, as we advanced, the natives left their villages, and retired to the hills, carrying all their cattle and effects with them, not being quite sure whether we were friends or foes.

September 22.—The place we arrived at this day is called Gutta, where there is a very large garrison, built upon the top of an immense rock, somewhat resembling that of Edinburgh Castle, but much higher. It was formerly one of Tippoo's towers of refuge; and was taken by the British with great difficulty. We halted here until we should get a reinforcement from Bombay, which was ordered to join us before we marched any farther. We were accord-

* These bandies are a kind of cart for the baggage, drawn by two bullocks.

ingly joined by his Majesty's 34th and 86th regiments, and also the 3d, 6th, and 9th regiments of native infantry, together with a large park of artillery from the island of Ceylon.

We now presented to the eye a very formidable appearance; and, humanly speaking, it would have taken a considerable force to have opposed our progress, being in all ten thousand King's and Company's troops. The followers of the army in this country are generally about four to one; so that, in all, we must have been in number about fifty thousand, white and black. Those who follow the army for a living, are washermen, (for it is the men, and not the women, who wash the clothes in this country,) barbers, cooly-boys, (that is, bearers of burdens, cooks' assistants, officers' under servants, &c.) dooly-bearers, horse-keepers, grass-cutters, officers' butlers, dubashes, and mati-boys, palanquin-bearers, lascars, for pitching the officers' tents, hospital-dressers, elephant-keepers, bandy-men, camel and bullock drivers, and bazaar people, who sold articles, such as rice cakes, spices, eggs, fowls, butcher meat, butter, &c. when they were to be obtained; but this was very frequently not the case, as I have before hinted; and in this case we were obliged to confine ourselves to our regimental allowances, which was very poor living for such laborious work.

September 29.—We were ordered to move forward. Our mode of marching was the following:—If our journey was long, we generally marched about three o'clock A. M., that we might have it over before the heat of the day; and we were allowed just half an hour to put on our clothes, strike our tents, and place them on the elephants, one of which was appointed to each company; and in that space of time our bandies had to be packed, and the army ready to march,—so you may see that we were not idle. We had mutton and rice twice a-day. The rice was carried upon bullocks, and the sheep driven along with us, and killed when we came to the ground which we were appointed to occupy for a night. We were sometimes nine hours upon the march, although we frequently did not travel above sixteen miles in the course of that time; and this you need not wonder at, for our roads (when we had any) were miserably bad and narrow, being generally confined by jungles on both sides, so that, with such a numerous body, moving forward frequently only two men deep, it was impossible for us to travel otherwise than at a very slow and interrupted pace; yet, although we were thus long upon our journey, we were sometimes two or three hours at our camp ground before we got our breakfast. But this hard marching, (I call it hard, for it was much worse than if we had been moving at an ordinary pace,) I say, this hard marching, and long abstinence, cut off great numbers of men; for we left them upon the road almost daily, both white and black.

I now experienced the great benefit of having a healthy active woman for the partner of my toils; for she used to go on before the regiment along with the cooks, and by the time the army was up, she would have gathered sticks, and found water for the tea-kettle, so that as soon as the elephants (who followed in the rear of the army) appeared with the tents, and ours was pitched, she would have our breakfast ready. It was my province to *forage* for rice cakes when I could get them to buy, which I did generally the night before, carrying them along with me, with some sugar and a bowl, tied up in my straw hat; and often, often have we sat down upon the ground, as contented in these circumstances, and much more so, than many of your European epicures with all their luxuries. Hunger and contentment made it sweet; for, as the Spirit of God by Solomon says, "Better is a dry morsel, and quietness therewith, than a house full of sacrifices with strife." There was just one thing that somewhat abated our relish for these comforts, and that was, to see the rest of the poor fellows in the tent hungry, as well as fatigued, while we could do very little for such a number. We always travelled bare-footed, as it would have been impossible for us to have procured shoes upon a march of this kind, travelling through so much water and sand alternately; for wherever there was any cultivation, the rice fields being for the most of the year flooded with water, the roads near them were generally rendered an absolute puddle. I may obseıve here, that travelling in this country is more severe in some respects for fair people than for those of a dark complexion; at least I have often had my face, feet, and even hands, blistered as if they had been scalded with boiling water; while I never saw any of our men of a dark complexion suffer in the same manner; and this accounts perhaps in no small degree, for fair people not retaining the impression of a warm climate so deeply as persons who are darker; for when these blisters disappear, the skin underneath is always renewed, and consequently continues fairer than if it had been exposed to the sun for a great length of time. At this time we had no knowledge where we were going, but, like Abraham, we went we knew not whither; for our Colonel, as I stated before, having the command of this division of the army, received his orders daily by the Tapaals (letter-carriers) from the Madras government.

October 1.—We fell in with a fine stream in the neighbourhood of some immense rocks, piled one above another in such a manner, that had it not been for their prodigious weight and size, I would have been tempted to believe they had been placed there by the hand of art. I am not at all surprised, that persons who live in such a temperate climate as ours, do not see the full force or beauty of many of the figures in the sacred volume; but were they to travel a few hundred miles in this country, they probably would not read their Bibles with such cold indifference; and, although even the figures of Scripture may fall short of the truth they are intended to convey, yet their appropriateness is often much greater than is generally conceived.

Were a reader of the Bible to see a company of way-worn travellers, whose feet were roasted with the burning sand of the desert, the sweat streaming from their bodies, and their features distorted with thirst and fatigue, running to those rocks and waters for cooling and refreshment, would he not then discover a sufficient illustration, both of the strength and sublimity at least, of the second clause in that passage of the prophet Isaiah, "A man shall be as a hiding-place from the wind, and a covert from the tempest; *as rivers of water in a dry place, and as the shadow of a great rock in a weary land.*"—And I am sure the traveller himself must be destitute of all moral taste or natural sensibility, or rather, in more appropriate language, "the things of the Spirit of God must be foolishness unto him," if he does not perceive the full force of this passage. I can say it from my repeated experience, that I have been so exhausted by heat, fatigue, and thirst, as to be hardly able to crawl along on the march, even with all the natural spirit I could muster; but after having had an opportunity of resting for a short season in the cleft or shadow of a large rock, and receiving a mouthful of refreshing water, I have gone forward more invigorated, than if I had partaken of the choicest dainties of India. Oh! that the blood and righteousness of Jesus Christ were as much valued by my precious and immortal soul, as the waters and rocks of the desert have been by my poor exhausted bodily frame! Oh, how precious indeed would he then be! I might then say with truth, that "he is the chiefest amongst ten thousand, and altogether lovely."

I would here remark, by the way, that there are many things in Scripture that were cleared up to me in this country, which before were quite unintelligible, and that circumstance rendered me so careless in reading my Bible. I shall mention one or two, which may suffice:—for instance, our Saviour says, "No man putteth new wine into old bottles, if otherwise, the bottles burst and the wine is spilled; but men put new wine into new bottles, and both are preserved." Now, I was wont to think that old bottles were not worse than new ones, if they were properly cleansed; but, when I saw the bottles of the east, made of the skins of animals sewed together, and of various sizes, I formed another opinion; for I saw that after these leathern bottles were in use for some time, the seams were very apt to give way, and our Saviour's words would be realized.

Another expression which puzzled me was this, "No man seweth a piece of new cloth upon an old garment, else the new piece that filled it up, *taketh away from the old,* and the rent is made worse."—With regard to this, I thought I had seen the tailor, when I was with my grandfather, making a very good job of an old coat, by mending it with new cloth; but when I saw the thin cotton garments of India, worn to a cob-web, I was then satisfied that he would be a clever artist indeed, that could sew a piece of new cotton cloth, however fine, to a spider's web, without tearing it in pieces.

Once more, and I shall have done; the apostle says, in the thirteenth of First Corinthians, "Now we see through a glass darkly, but then face to face:" Now, I could not perceive the fitness of this figure, as people use a glass, or glasses, to enable them to see better; but when I saw the glass of the east, (and I suppose in the country and age of the apostle it was similar,) I say, when I saw the glass here, made of paste from rice-flour, blown and fired, my opinion was entirely changed, as it is quite dim, and full of white scales; so that, if persons look through it, they observe objects as the blind man did, mentioned in the gospel, who, when his sight was only in part restored, said that he saw "men like trees walking." I could bring forward many other passages, but I give you these as specimens; and, to deal plainly with you, my dear reader, I must tell you that I was very little short of a Deist before the Lord brought me here; because, as I could not see how this and the other thing could be, I in a manner rejected them as false, or at least gave myself very little concern about them; but when such things as these were made out to me, I then perceived that it was in consequence of the blindness of my mind, and not from the want of truth and evidence in the Bible, that I was not able to understand such difficulties; and, by the blessing of God, I gradually conceived a greater and a greater liking for that best of books, which alone points out to sinful men the way of salvation.

October 12.—We encamped this day at a place called Canool. This is a beautiful country, and abounds with woods and water, the river Tamboothera running close by the town. We had here a visit of the Nabob of Canool, with an equipage nearly resembling that of the Nabob of the Poligar country, formerly described. While we were upon the banks of this river, the artillery from Ceylon, his Majesty's 66th and 89th regiments left us, on account of a general order received to that effect. As the rebels had given up Seringapatam and other forts which they had in possession, when they heard of such a powerful army coming against them; and Colonel Bell, with a number of other European officers of different ranks in the Company's service were taken into custody, and sent prisoners to Madras; this business, therefore, terminated much more favourably than was expected; for the 25th light dragoons was, I may say, the only European regiment that suffered any thing by powder and shot; but although there were comparatively few lives lost in this way, yet during the march a great number indeed, both white and black, went to their long homes. I dare say it, from my own observation and inquiry, that there is an average of ten men who die from the fatigues and disorders incident to this country, to one that dies by the fate of war.

October 16.—We crossed the river Tamboothera in what may be with justice termed basket boats. These boats were made by strong twigs interwoven with each other, and covered externally with buffalo hides. They were of a circular form, and managed by short flat paddles, and without any helm; each boat containing 12 or 14 men with their firelocks and knapsacks. Our baggage and bandies were also carried over in them, but the cattle of every kind were obliged to swim. It was truly amusing to see the elephants and bullocks get across, for the elephants being driven to the side of the river, entered and swam over, holding up their trunks all the while for the sake of air; but there was one of them that would not take the water in spite of all the efforts the keepers could use, and at last they compelled him, by bringing out two lusty ones of his kindred tribe, who, at the command of their drivers, fairly pushed him into the water by main force with their heads. The bullocks were led two and two by their driver, who went before them lying upon a plank previously tied to his body, holding a rope which was fastened at each end to the horns of his cattle; one man thereby moving himself and leading his bullocks by the motion of his feet. We were two days in gètting ourselves, with the baggage and cattle, across this river, and we pitched upon the right bank for one night.

October 19—. We reached the left bank of the Kistna. This river is larger than the former, and the same boats were carried from the Tamboothera by three coolies, or labourers, to each boat, and we crossed in the manner formerly described. Upon this camp ground, I got (what is called in English) a live grass in the fleshy part of my leg. This grass has much the resemblance of a bear or barley awn, and is furnished with a small barb at the one end, like that of a fish hook; and when it once enters the flesh, there is hardly a possibility of extracting it. It takes its name from the motion it exhibits when laid upon the hand, because it is twisted, and when pulled from the stalk the twist goes out and produces a motion like a hard twisted cord. I have heard many strange stories about this live grass, as of its entering at the one side of the foot or leg, and working its way to the other, and in consequence of its poisonous qualities that many have died thereby. But I shall not affirm these things for truth, as I never saw any such fatal effects produced by it; but this I know, that all I received from the doctor did not cure it; and the wound in the course of a week became quite black, and was attended with a considerable degree of pain, which was probably much aggravated by our severe marches. But when we arrived at Hydrabad, and I was seized with the jungle fever, the leg was totally neglected, I may say, and when I recovered from this disorder, we were quite surprised to find the wound healed. For this I had great reason to be thankful, as I have known instances of death being indirectly produced by still more trifling causes. Some of our men, for example, may be said to have died of the bite of a mosquito, for the bite of that little insect occasioned a grievous itch, and the part being constantly scratched, soon festered and mortified, so that it was necessary to cut off the leg, after which the poor men fevered and died.

I would remark, by the way, that there are a great number of annoyances to the poor soldier in this country, exclusive of hard marching, bad provisions, wet camp ground, and the many bodily afflictions arising from the climate: because upon the march, they are liable to get bitten by serpents, or stung with scorpions and centipedes. And in all the barracks in the country that I have seen, or heard of, they are infested with bugs, in such a degree as often compels the men to take to the barrack square, and to sleep under the canopy of heaven, by which means, while seeking to avoid one evil, they expose themselves to a worse, for the heavy dews during night are almost sure to bring on the flux, the most fatal of all the disorders of this country.

October 23.—Upon this march one of our sepoys was bitten by a green snake. This poor man suffered the most agonizing pain which I suppose is possible for a mortal to endure, but his sufferings were soon terminated in this world, for he expired in a few hours. The green snake is thought to be the most dangerous of all the serpent tribe in this country. I have never known nor ever heard of a person recovering that had been bitten. It takes its name from its green colour, and it generally frequents fertile places, where it is not easily perceived, which makes it still more dangerous. It will not, however, attack any person unless he treads upon it, or approaches very near its young. It is about the length and thickness of a coachman's whip. The influence which the Great Enlivener of animal and vegetable life exercises upon this animal is most remarkable, for while it is exposed to the sun's rays, it seems almost impossible to deprive it totally of life. I had this information from a very intelligent native, who also showed me one that he had been endeavouring to kill, but to no purpose; for after he had bruised the head to pieces, it was still in motion when I saw it, at which time the sun was a little past his meridian, but this glorious luminary had not finished his daily course many minutes when all signs of life and motion completely vanished.

Many of the serpent tribe here are perfectly harmless to man, and may even be tamed so as to act the part of a cat in destroying vermin. The tanks, or ponds, are full of water snakes, which, when bathing, we often amused ourselves with endeavouring to catch, and never received the least injury from any of them. There is a land snake, however, called the *Hooded*, or *spectacle* snake, (from the appearance of a pair of spectacles on the back part of the head,) the bite of which is very deadly, but even of these I have seen great numbers tamed, and carried about in baskets through the barracks, by the natives, for a kind of livelihood. No sooner was the basket uncovered, and the owner commenced playing on his simple instrument, than it raised its head and moved it about with all the gestures of a coxcomb possessed of a new suit of clothes and a silver-headed cane; but when the charmer desisted from his playing, the snake generally made a dart at him, which he studiously avoided, and pretended to be very much afraid of, but this was just a pretence for making us wonder, for it could do no harm, being previously deprived of the sting, or rather the bag of poison, which lies within its mouth.

Although serpents generally love music, yet here, as in most other cases, there are exceptions to the general rule; for I am told there is one species, which, instead of being allured by the charms of music, testifies a very remarkable aversion to it; and we need not wonder at this peculiarity, for we know that, generally speaking, all the human species, whether civilized or savage, are fond of music: but we know also that there are many individuals to whom it is rather an annoyance than a pleasure. The serpent I have alluded to is probably the species which the Psalmist had in his eye, when he compared wicked men to it, in respect of their dislike and antipathy to divine truth. It has been said, indeed, that there is a serpent, or adder, to which the Psalmist's comparison literally applies; that it actually covers one ear with its tail, and applies the other close upon the ground, to prevent itself being overcome with the charms of music, so as to run the hazard of being taken and killed. We know certainly, both from Scripture and observation, that the serpent is subtile above all beasts of the field, but this surely is a piece of cunning which is beyond its nature. It is surely much more rational to think that the Psalmist refers entirely to the utter dislike of the charmer and his music, which this serpent is characterized by; and, moreover, we have the words "stoppeth his ears," in Isaiah xxxiii. 15, employed to express the utmost disregard and abhorrence.

CHAPTER VI.

November 3.—We marched past Hydrabad, the capital of the prince of Nizam's dominions, and pitched our camp at Secundrabad, which is six miles distant, where there are barracks for European troops, which at this time were occupied by his Majesty's 33d regiment. The country being now tolerably quiet, a general order came for our regiment to take the duty of Secundrabad, and the other regiments were appointed also to different stations: so the 33d marched out to our camp ground, and we took possession of their barracks, after a march of three months, halting days included. But though our march was now over, its sad effects were not over; for a great proportion of our men were seized with what is called the jungle fever. This fever some say is occasioned by an unwholesome moisture exhaled by the sun out of the jungles or bushes through which we had marched; others, that it is totally owing to the excessive fatigues, and want of proper nourishment, to which the soldiers were exposed in this country; but as I am no student of physic, I cannot say what the real causes were, but this I know from experience, that its effects were very deplorable; for I also was seized with it at this time, and was despaired of by the doctor. It is attended with great pain in the head and excessive vomiting, insomuch that a person looking upon one labouring under this disorder would be apt to think he could not live many minutes. My wife had a great deal of fatigue with me while ill of this fever, which lasted about a fortnight; but, by the blessing of God on the use of means, and particularly by the singular care and attention of this most valuable partner in all my troubles, I recovered. Had I been sent to the hospital, and received no better attendance than it was possible for the men to obtain there, I would in all probability have shared their fate.

While we lay here, some of our men were bitten by a mad dog, two of whom died shortly after; but the doctors took rather a strange method with the third. A corporal was ordered to attend him from morning to night, and to carry him out to the fields and villages to amuse his mind, and to give him as much liquor as would keep him always in a kind of intoxicated state. Now, whether it was the effect of the liquor in preventing his mind from dwelling upon his dangerous situation, or whether the operation of the liquor destroyed the effect of the bite, or (what is as likely perhaps) that the poison had not been sufficiently strong in his body to produce fatal consequences, I will not attempt

corps; and this piece of voluntary attention on the part of my wife the poor fellow never could forget. Whatever he could give her, or do for her, he seemed to think all too little for her kindness; and to me he was every thing that was tractable and attentive. But the reason of my mentioning this boy more than any other of my acquaintance who died at this time, is, upon the account of the singular regard he shewed for his Bible, and the extraordinary circumstances by which it seems to have been excited; which I hope my reader will not find fault with me for particularly noticing.

One day, about the commencement of his fatal disorder, which was a flux, he was at the *common* place for the men, and our drum-major, and another young man of the name of Gardiner, happened to be there at the same time. These two fell into a strange and fearful discourse respecting their trouble, and the likely termination of it. Says the drum-major to Gardiner,

"You are bad of the flux too, I see." To which Gardiner replied, "D——d bad, drum-major." "Well, so am I, and we will both die, and go to h—ll, but you will die first; and, remember, you are to come and meet me half way."

The poor lad came into our room, much alarmed, and told us the woful story; but he was much more so when they both died, and in the order predicted by the drum-major; but whether they went to hell, or whether the one met the other half-way, is not my business to determine; but this I say, from the infallible word of the Lord, "that the wicked shall be turned into hell, and all they that forget God." The trouble both of mind and body of this boy still increasing, his love for his Bible increased with it; for he was fully persuaded, that his Bible alone could tell him how to avoid that dreadful place of which his fears had been awakened, and likewise point out to him how he could be happy after death. A day or two before he died,

I went to the hospital, to inquire how he was. I found him drawing near the close of life; but his complaints were not so much of his pain as of his being deprived of all means of reading the Bible, on account of the dimness of his sight, in consequence of his trouble. His comrade being permitted to be with him for some days before his death, I proposed that he should read to him sometimes; but at these words, Wilkins burst into tears, and being asked the reason, said, that it was because his comrade had never learned to read that blessed book. He still continued to get worse, until he died; but he would never part with his Bible, (although he returned to me Mr. Boston's Fourfold State, which I had lent him,) but kept it under his pillow, or hugged it in his bosom until he expired.

A few months after we came to Secundrabad, an order came for four companies of our regiment to proceed to Masulipatam, to do the duty of that place, and, amongst these was my good hospital friend, Alexander Chevis, for the which I was very sorry ; but in a few months afterwards we received a route for the same place, to embark for *foreign* service, as every departure from India, for any island or country under the British government is called.

There is just one circumstance, which I will mention before I take my leave of this place, which appears fully as important to myself as any thing I have seen or experienced since I came to it; and it is this: —I had frequently been in heaviness, through manifold temptations, in consequence of my remaining ignorance, and corresponding want of faith, since my blessed affliction in the Prince of Wales's Island, and particularly after my kind instructor A. C. left the regiment with his company for Masulipatam, for I then lost him who had formerly "comforted me in all my tribulations, with that comfort wherewith he himself had been comforted of God;" but here I again found, as I had often formerly done, the loving kindness of the Lord, in a gracious providence, for he provided relief for me from a quarter whence I could have very little expected it, as I shall now relate:—

There was a person in the regiment, of the name of Serjeant Gray, with whom I had hitherto a very slender acquaintance. He was a married man, and I had never seen any thing but what led me to believe that he and his wife were what are generally called very decent, well-behaved people; though, whether they were at all concerned about religion or not, was a matter I was entirely ignorant of; but one day, when I was in a very melancholy mood, I thought I would go over to their barrack-room, and get a little social converse with them, to cheer me, which I accordingly did, and found only Mrs. Gray at home, industriously engaged in sewing. After having made inquiry for each other's welfare, I said it was a pity that there was no such thing as getting any good books, when a person had a little spare time, to improve his mind. She said it was, but immediately added, that she had at present the loan of what she thought a very excellent book, belonging to one of the men. I, somewhat eagerly, expressed a desire to see it, which she instantly complied with; but how was my astonishment excited, when I found it to be a book that my grandfather highly respected, and expressed his esteem for it by saying, that if he was condemned to spend the remainder of his earthly pilgrimage in an uninhabited island, like the Apostle John, and had it in his power to choose a few books to take along with him, the next he would select after his Bible, would be Doddridge's Rise and Progress of Religion in the Soul. In the circumstances in which I was at that moment placed, I need scarcely give the Christian reader any unnecessary information, in saying, that "I rejoiced like one who had found great spoil." I then made so free with Mrs. Gray as to ask her to which of the men it belonged, and if she would let me have it for a day or two, that I might peruse it? She said I was very welcome to do that, and also told me who was the proprietor; but if I went to see her with a heavy heart, I returned home with a light one, for I was so overjoyed that I hardly knew that my weak limbs had a body to support. I had heard, as I have already said, that there was such a book existing, but I had never inquired after it when I could have made it my own, nor ever had seen it until this happy hour; and little could I have expected to find it in this wilderness, where, alas! there were no refreshing waters to satisfy the longing desires of a thirsty soul; and this book, I think, of all other human compositions I have yet known, was best adapted to my condition; neither is it necessary to add, that I read it over again and again, until I had almost the whole substance of those parts of it by heart which more immediately corresponded with the present state of my mind, and with my former experience. I must be plain enough to say, that I did not desire to keep this book altogether to myself, but wished also that others might derive benefit from its contents; but this I will also state, that I thought I would be a man possessed of great wealth if I could call it my own. I therefore inquired at the person to whom it belonged if he was disposed to part with it, and if so, that I would give him whatever price he would ask. He said that I was welcome to have it for sixteen finams, (about three shillings.) I therefore closed with him immediately for that small sum. I was now blessed with ample means of instruction, and I would indulge a hope that I was not only made wiser by it, but I trust also better, by the blessing of God upon my search after truth, and that it has not been to me the savour of death unto death, but the savour of life unto life. I shall add no more at present respecting this excellent work, as I shall have occasion to speak of it again.

CHAPTER VII.

We left Secundrabad on the 11th February, 1811, and proceeded, by forced marches, to Masulipatam, where I had not long been when I was again thrown into a very disordered state, in consequence of the hot winds, being so ill with my breathing that my wife was under the necessity of fanning me during two whole days. After I recovered, there being some of my fifers in the hospital, I went in one day to see how they were getting on; and, to my great astonishment, as I entered the hospital, whom did I see there but my dear friend Alexander Chevis, lying like a skeleton in one of the cots. I looked at him for some time before I could believe my own eyes; and scarcely being yet sure, I said to him, "Sandy, is this you?" He answered in the affirmative. After having inquired into all particulars, and conversed a little with him, I immediately went home and described to my wife the situation of this good man; and we set about concerting measures that might in some degree mitigate his distresses,—for he was at this time far gone in the complaint under which I laboured, when he was "God's hand" in comforting and instructing me; and truly I saw here a divine call, as well as the call of a grateful heart, considering what he had done for me in Prince of Wales's Island.

Whenever my duty would permit, I was consequently in the hospital, reading and conversing with him; and on the two Sabbaths that he lived after this, I remained with him nearly the whole day; but my attendance on him was richly rewarded, for I learned more from this dying saint of what is really worth learning, than I had done all my life before.

A few nights before he died, he expressed a desire that I should bring my wife, and Serjeant Gray with his wife, who had formerly been friendly to him, that he might have the satisfaction of seeing us altogether before he departed, the which I did; and he had saved some of his daily allowance of wine, that we might all drink before him, and appear comfortable. When we were all seated, and had ate and drank together, he expressed himself in nearly the following words:—"My dear friends, although I may never again see you in this world, I wish that the keeper of Israel may keep you from falling before the many temptations to which you are exposed, and bless you, and preserve to his heavenly kingdom; and, although in all probability we shall never behold each other in the face, while here, I pray that the Lord may seal you among his treasures, and make you his, in the day when he maketh up his jewels."

When I went next morning to inquire how he had rested, he told me he had been very much pained, and appeared to be going very fast. I spent as much of the day with him as my duty would permit, and when I went at night with his drop of punch, which we used to make for him, and which he preferred to the hospital wine, I found him somewhat easier; but he said to me, he felt he had but a very short time to live; so I took an affectionate farewell of him, but in the morning he was still living. He told me he had been much worse during the night, and had suffered great pain, and added, "that he had a desire to depart from a sinful heart, a wicked world, and a loathsome disease, and to be with Christ, where holiness dwells, where sin shall never enter, and where the inhabitants shall no more say, I am sick." So the Lord granted his petition, for he died that evening. "Lord enable me to live the life, that I may die the death, of the righteous, and that my last end may be like his!"

We remained in Masulipatam about four months, and I was very glad to hear when the route came for us to leave it; for it was not only intolerably hot, but when it blew, we were like to be suffocated with clouds of sand; and it was the worst place for provisions we had yet seen. The butcher meat was so very bad that we had it only once within our door all that time. But I would have been happy indeed had this march been to embark for Europe; for the regiment was getting daily more and more profligate and abominable! Here the papists laid a plot for destroying the protestants, but it was detected, and the ringleaders punished; and here, too, the men were shooting themselves, or one another, whenever the freak took them.

We had a young fellow of the name of Courtney, who shot two men with one ball in the open barrack room! one of them was a man belonging to the regiment, and the other a black man, who was in the barrack selling cloth for a livelihood. The white man had been impeaching Courtney with stealing something from him, which the other flatly denied, though falsely, (at least he was a noted thief,) and threatened to make him repent it; and in the course of a little time afterward, he took down his firelock, and pretended to be spunging her out, no one ever in the least suspecting him to be putting in a ball-cartridge out of his pouch; so he levelled her for the person whom he had just been threatening, and sent the contents through his body, and they lodged also in that of the black man. Both of them died in a very short time. He was immediately taken into confinement, and in a short time was sent to Madras, where he was tried, convicted, and executed. But, to show the hardened character of this faithful servant of Satan, I may mention, that one of the soldiers asked him, before he left the regiment, "if he was not sorry for what he had done?" to which he replied, "that what he was most sorry for was, that *he could not get an hour's fowling in the barracks before he went away!*" What think you of this in a youth of nineteen years of age! I doubt not but it will strike the mind of the reader at once, what a contrast there was between him and my dear deceased friend just now mentioned; but the "tares and the wheat must grow together until the harvest," when an eternal separation shall take place; for those of similar dispositions shall then come together, never, never more to be separated! Oh! comforting to think that there shall not be one sinner in the vast congregation of the righteous. For the righteous who have here the image of God partially restored, shall then "shine as the sun" in the kingdom of their father.

As I have been speaking of shooting, I must mention one other circumstance before I leave this bloody subject, which is of the wonderful kind; for in the former case, we see or hear of one man killing two of his fellow-creatures with one ball; now I am going to tell you of another that had two balls through him and yet lived!—

Our men were in general very profligate with the native women, and one of them having a quarrel with his black concubine, was resolved to give her the effectual cure for a bad wife; and, to accomplish his purpose, he put two ball-cartridges into his firelock, and laid her quietly out of the way, until an opportunity would present itself to shoot her; and when she made her appearance, while he was in the act of raising the gun, one of his comrades, who knew of his diabolical design, made an attempt to wrest the firelock from him, but, in the scuffle, some of their feet touching the trigger, the firelock exploded, and both of the balls went through his body. This is the most wonderful accident of this kind I have ever known, for this man was at his duty in about six weeks afterwards! And the wonder lies chiefly in considering that the balls entered his belly and came out at his back.

There was a black nabob also made away with himself here. He was sent down the country to the charge of our regiment for not paying his tribute; but, laying this treatment very much to heart, he fell into a state of melancholy, and put an end to his existence by means of a knife, having given the guard that was over him a wedge of gold the day before.

In giving this sad picture of the wickedness of the regiment, some of my readers may think I have been guilty of exaggeration. They may say, we have heard of soldiers being given to drinking and swearing, and all manner of debauchery; but surely when you tell us that they were given to such things as shooting themselves, or one another, it must certainly be one of those extraordinary stories that travellers are so often accused of telling, in order to excite one's astonishment. But I can assure you I have related nothing but facts, and many more I could give you as horrible as those above mentioned. Though I have little inclination for the task, I will enter a little more into the subject, pointing out some of the circumstances which brought about this deplorable state of things, and illustrate the progress of sin by one or two individual examples which came under my own notice. Should any of my readers be touched to the quick by any thing I shall write; that is, should they trace in the characters I may bring forward any resemblance to their own, let them not turn away from comparing likenesses. If you are still under the power of sin, you are the enemy of God, and carry about with you the same principle of depravity which operated in these men, and produced such woful effects. Therefore, "be not high-minded, but fear." "For as in water face answers to face, so does the heart of man to man."

On the other hand, if you have a scriptural ground of hope that you are turned from darkness to light, and from the dominion of sin and Satan unto God; you may be led by a consideration of these things to give him all the glory, for unto him it belongs. "For who maketh thee to differ from another, and what hast thou which thou didst not receive? therefore, glory not as thou hadst not received it." But rather let you and I join with the Psalmist, in a tribute of praise unto him who has delivered us from becoming the prey of the terrible, saying, "Not unto us, O Lord, not unto us, but unto thy name give the glory, for thy mercy, and for thy truth's sake."

I have already said, that upon the march we endured great fatigues, and also many inconveniencies; but, when in barracks, a soldier's life in India is commonly very easy. They have not unfrequently eight or nine successive nights in bed; and, as the climate is generally very dry, they are not liable to get their arms or accoutrements often wet; and many of them likewise keep black boys to clean their things, take their victuals upon guard, and relieve them of other labours. They had consequently much spare time which they did not know how to get rid off; "and an idle man (says Mr. Bucke) is his own tormentor, always full of wants and complaints; while his inactivity often proves fatal both to his body and his mind. The worst importunities, the most embarrassing perplexities of business, are softness and luxury, compared with the incessant cravings of vacancy, and the unsatisfactory expedients of idleness." It is a saying among the Turks, that a "busy man is troubled with one devil, but the idle man with twenty."

The want of exercise for both body and mind therefore, and the natural consequences of a sultry climate upon the constitution, rendered a soldier's life in these circumstances truly a burden, for he was unable to walk abroad through the day

6

because of the intense heat, and, moreover, the regiment was not unfrequently confined to barracks, on account of their misconduct. Now, if you consider such numbers of men as I formerly mentioned living together in one barrack-room, some sleeping away their time*, and others lounging about the piazzas, not knowing what to do with themselves, you will not find much difficulty in perceiving that these poor creatures were eminently exposed to become the prey of him that "walketh about as a roaring lion, seeking whom he may devour." Those, on the other hand, who were disposed to improve their time, by reading their Bibles†, or conversing upon religious or useful subjects, were disturbed

* I would here remark, that sleeping in the day is very dangerous in that country, for I have often known men lying down upon their cots to take a nap in perfect health, that would rise in the rage of a fever, and were obliged to be taken to the hospital.

† Those who had not Bibles of their own, had access to the Company's Bibles, which were served out to us before embarking at Portsmouth.

by the devil's agents, even those who "were led captive by him at his will;" for when these debauched beings, in their rambles, observed any of their comrades thus employed, they would make up a plot to annoy them, by singing obscene songs, cursing and swearing in their very ears, or by tumbling one another in a riotous manner upon these *Sammy Hawks* *, as they were called. This species of persecution being frequently repeated, we may wonder the less that those who had not the root of the matter in them, were discouraged, and, in this time of temptation, fell away; and that, in process of time,

* The *Sammy Hawk* is a kind of brown bird that frequently flies about the barracks, to pick up any thing that it can find for its subsistence; and it has a kind of religious homage paid to it by some of the poor, ignorant natives. The meaning this nickname was intended to convey was, that those to whom it was applied were men of sober habits, who had not the heart to spend their money in the same jovial manner as their thoughtless comrades, who were determined, therefore, if they saved their money, that it should not be with both ease and honour.

instead of reading their Bibles, or conversing upon religious subjects, they preferred taking a cheerful glass together, which would at once relieve them from such assaults, enliven that gloom which brooded over their minds, transport them in imagination to Glasgow*, to see how the shuttle was flying, and afterwards to close the scene with their favourite song,

"Glasgow on the banks of the river Clyde."

In this way many of those who might be called the sober and decent part of the regiment, gradually fell from their steadfastness, and became as dissipated as those whom they had condemned. From the miserable languor produced by idleness and the climate, they now did not bethink themselves of any other refuge than liquor; *mustering a fuddle* as often as possible; which is by two or three of them clubbing toge-

* A great proportion of the regiment had been enlisted in that city, and its neighbourhood.

ther for a rupee's worth of arrack*; and it was no uncommon thing to hear it said, on these occasions, that it was of no use for them to lay up money for others to spend; and as their comrades were dying so fast, and they did not know how soon it would be their turn, it was the best way to be

* Two drams of arrack were served out daily to each of the men, and as there were at that time no canteens in the regiment, the jovial fellows could not obtain more than their allowance but by getting it from the women, the *Sammy Hawks,* or from such of their boon companions who had *put in the pin or kegged,* which expressions signify to take an oath against liquor till some given time, such as the new year's day, the king's birth day, some particular fair in their native place. From the regimental store nothing beyond the ordinary allowance could be obtained but by *drawing out a chit* or line, and having it subscribed by the commanding officer, addressed to the keeper of the store, who delivered the quantity specified upon receiving payment for it; but it required a very sufficient reason indeed; such as a marriage, the baptism of a child, or something of that nature, before our Colonel would subscribe such an order. I understand that canteens are now common in every barrack in India, from the belief that the men will not be so mad upon liquor when they have the power to spend their money as they think proper.

merry when they had it in their power; saying in effect, "Let us eat and drink, for to-morrow we die." In their drunken rambles they would often have altercations amongst themselves, or with the noncommissioned officers, when trying to keep good order amongst them, which brought them under one or more breaches of the articles of war; and this not unfrequently terminated in their pain and dishonour, by their being exposed to corporal punishment in the front of the regiment. To those who had any regard to their good name, this was a severe trial, and the effect generally was, that it either cast them into a despondency of mind, or more commonly rendered them utterly regardless of their character ever afterwards.

I may also notice a circumstance which had not a little influence in spreading this evil contagion amongst us.

After we crossed the equinoctial line, going to India, it was the notion of a number, even of the men who seemed to have had something like religious instruction, that they were then under no obligations to keep the sabbath, saying, that there was no sabbath beyond the line. This sentiment became a matter of frequent discussion amongst many of them, and seemed to receive a very welcome reception. I could not suppose that they were in earnest in this opinion, until they manifested by their conduct either that they really believed it, or that they had succeeded in silencing their conscience on the subject; for, after passing the line, they made no scruple whatever of whistling and singing, and passing the sabbath day in vain and unprofitable discourse, if not in profane talking and jesting. On their arrival in India, their notions were still farther confirmed by the irreligious and profane example set before them by our countrymen of all ranks. As they were in a land of heathens they thought they had liberty to live as heathens. The contagion spread rapidly in the regiment, and cast down many wounded; and not a few of those whom I thought to be strong men were slain by it.

The Apostolic injunction against the dangerous consequences of evil principle and evil example is, "Be not deceived, evil communications corrupt good manners." I will now, as I promised, illustrate these remarks by one or two examples, and Oh! how it pains me to think that ever I should have it in my power to draw these illustrations from the conduct of those whom I once loved; but I hope my reader will not blame me, as what I shall mention now cannot disturb the mouldering ashes of my once dear companions, and as their names shall be concealed, lest it might give a wound to the hearts of their relatives, if this little work should come in their way, which nothing could heal.

The reasons I select the following persons in preference to many others are, first, that I was intimately acquainted with them, and am, therefore, under no hazard of being led into any mistake about what I am going to write; and the other is, that when I see this, I may remember my former dangerous situation, and have something before me well calculated to excite my thankfulness to that Power, who has preserved me from being wrecked upon those rocks, which dashed them to pieces.

The reader may recollect that I was formerly a fifer in the grenadier company of the 26th Regiment, and also that there were a great number of the men took the bounty from that corps and went to the Royals. While I was in that company and regiment I had a young man for my comrade, whom I shall call J. F. who was a man of very sober habits, being given to none of those vices for which soldiers are remarkable; nay, he was even so much averse to swearing, that he used to reprove me frequently for making use of what are generally termed minced oaths, to which I was then much addicted, but by means of his repeated friendly and seasonable admonitions, I was at last enabled to leave them off. After we came to India, however, he attached himself to some of those men who had imbibed the libertine principles mentioned above, and with these "evil men and seducers, he waxed worse and worse, deceiving and being deceived." Solomon's question is a pertinent one: "Can a man carry fire in his bosom and his clothes not be burnt? Can a man walk upon hot coals and his feet not be burnt?" Alas, my poor friend soon forgot his own admonitions to me, about my swearing when in Dublin; and when I reminded him of them, he only laughed me to scorn; for the oaths I made use of at that time, when he acted so friendly a part in pointing out to me the evil of the practice, were to him now quite insignificant. Nothing, in regard to swearing, appeared to satisfy him now but the great and dreadful names of Jehovah, and those glorious attributes by which he makes himself known; nor was this all, for he became a mocker at every thing sacred, making himself acquainted with the word of God, for no other reason than as a storehouse whence he might amply supply himself with expressions which he could pervert to the purposes of buffoonery, and that he might be able to pour down vollies of raillery upon all those who had even but a small form of godliness*. To show you how far his wickedness carried him, I may mention, that at one time he and another of his lewd companions went at night to the hospital where a woman's husband was lying a corpse, and she sitting up with the remains of him who was once loved but now departed, each having a white sheet about him, to make the poor affrighted and rather superstitious female believe, that it was the husband returned from the other world, attended by some of his kindred spirits to pay her a visit, which almost put

* This puts me in mind of the saying of good Mr. Boston, with regard to people of this description.—"Those who act such a part," says he, "behave as foolishly, but more criminally, than that person who would dig into a mine for metal to melt and pour down his own and his neighbour's throat."

the poor woman out of her mind. This piece of barbarous conduct was made up, else it would have probably cost them both their serjeants' coats.

The reader may easily suppose that I had, long ere now, ceased to keep company with him; for all my attempts to show him the inconsistency and criminality of his conduct had long before this time proved useless. I therefore saw it to be my duty to keep at a distance from him, for the admonition is, "from such withdraw thyself."

To be short, he was seized by the flux in Trichinopoly, of which disorder he died. I have said that he had been long to me "as a heathen man and a publican;" but when I heard that he was dangerously ill, I was certainly very sorry for the poor lad, and went up as soon as I could find it convenient to see him, which was the night before we marched for Bangalore. I asked about his complaint, and if he thought he was getting any better. He said he was very ill, and not likely to get better.

Fain would I have spoken to him about his spiritual malady, which was my greatest concern, but I was afraid to be rash, lest he should take it rather as a reproach than as a friendly inquiry or salutary admonition, and therefore waited a little to see if he would break in upon the subject first. He was not long in partly relieving my anxiety, by saying, he had been a very wicked man. This he acknowledged in the general, and did not condescend to particulars; but in a very few words said he was afraid he would soon die; and, like most men who have led a wicked life, he added, that if he got better he would never be what he had been, and that he had been long J. F. but he would be so no longer. To which I answered, I hope you may not; but without strength to aid your resolutions, I am afraid there will be little change for the better; and having pointed him to the only refuge for sinners, even to him "who is able to save to the very uttermost," I left him: but how did it strike like a dart through my liver, when we arrived at the first camp ground from Trichinopoly, to hear that poor J. F. was no longer in the land of the living, and in the place of hope. This was truly a melancholy case, but I will not say that it was without hope, for he who saved one at the last hour, was able also to save him. But this is no encouragement for us "to continue in sin, that grace may abound." There is indeed *one* case mentioned in Scripture of a person being saved at the last hour, that none may despair, and *but one*, that none may presume. Ah! my dear reader, let not you and I hazard our eternal all on such an uncertainty, for these are dreadful words: "Because I have called, and ye refused; I have stretched out my hand, and no man regarded; but ye have set at nought all my counsel, and would none of my reproof; I also will laugh at your calamity; I will mock when your fear cometh: when your fear cometh as desolation, and your destruction cometh as a whirlwind; when distress and anguish cometh upon you. Then shall they call upon me, but I will not answer; they shall seek me early, but they shall not find me: for that they hated knowledge, and did not choose the fear of the Lord: they would have none of my counsel; they despised all my reproof: therefore shall they eat of the fruit of their own way, and be filled with their own devices." Now, "consider this, ye that forget God, lest he tear you in pieces when there is none to deliver."

The other person whom I shall mention was formerly a ploughman, and had enlisted into the army upon account of some love affair. While in the above capacity, he had formed an intimacy with his master's daughter; and, from what I could learn, they were remarkably attached to each other. But the father of the young woman directly opposing his parental authority to their union, the young man took it so much to heart, that he went and joined himself to a party of the Royal Scots as a private soldier; and by this step, he, like too many, punished himself for the fault of another.

My first acquaintance with W. H. was after we came to Wallajahbad; and we used to spend many a happy hour together when in barracks, and even upon the march, talking over old stories, and singing the songs of our native land,—"which softened our hardships,—cheered our lonely hearts,—brought to our recollection the images of those friends from whom we had departed, while fond hope whispered that we would yet revisit these scenes,—converse with these friends,—and renew these joys. In this sadly pleasing retrospect, and joyful anticipation, we lost the sense of our sorrows, and journeyed onward with increased vigour." Neither did the day of the Lord pass by us altogether unimproved; for then we used to meet together for religious conversation, and particularly upon the Sabbath evenings, when I was waiting for tatoo-beating, in the front of the barracks*. But, alas! poor man, he gra-

* The reader may quite naturally think that there was a great inconsistency displayed here; first talking of the religion of Jesus, and then rushing immediately into a breach of that sacred command, "Remember the Sabbath day to keep it holy;" now, was not playing on a musical instrument directly opposed to this precept? I answer that it certainly was; but you may believe me that it was necessity, and not choice on my part, that forced me to do it; and the first time I played the fife upon the Lord's day going to church, after I joined the 26th, I was in such a state of perturbation that I could not play a note, although I kept the fife to my mouth, and moved my fingers as if I was as busy as any of them. Thus we may see that although any sin may, upon its first commission, cause great pain to the conscience, yet the more frequently it is repeated, the more natural it becomes, for this uneasiness had left me long before the time I allude to. We had therefore much need to guard against sin in whatever form it appears, for it hath been justly said, that "he who despiseth small things shall fall by little and little;" but I am of opinion that the malignity of my crime consisted principally in not weighing these things, before I came into this state of subjection; for I was not ignorant that this was a part of a fifer's duty in the army; but although I will not attempt to justify my conduct; yet this I will say, that I could earnestly wish that my mind had been always as well

dually lost the relish for divine things, by forming a connexion with some debauched characters; and keeping company with these jovial fellows, as they are called, he soon became a very different man.

However, I never had reason to think, neither did I ever hear, that he was guilty of those enormities with which the other person has been too justly charged; and when I expostulated with him about his

employed when I have professedly been worshipping God, as it has been when engaged in this musical employment, after my blessed affliction in the Prince of Wales's Island; for I have often been so full of the topics we had been conversing about, as to be unable to know whether I was playing or not, until the rest of the corps, (as is common in these cases, after the tune is played over two or three times,) waited to hear if I was going to change it, and the sound thus dying away, it would immediately strike me that I was so engaged; and you may think it strange, when I tell you, that I never recollect in one instance of even making a mistake, for when I would come to myself, I was playing with the greatest fluency, although I acknowledge that I have been taken sometimes so short, that I was obliged to repeat the tune once more than I perhaps would have done, not being provided in my own mind with another in time.

conduct, he took it always apparently in good part, and promised to do better; but after repeatedly repenting in a kind of a way, and as often "returning like the dog to his vomit," he avoided my company altogether; and at any time when I went to see him, if he observed me coming in at one barrack-room door, he would immediately go out at another, being unable to answer to me for his conduct; and my presence grieved him, as it called to his mind the many happy hours of profitable and innocent enjoyment we had spent in one another's company. So true it is that guilt is a coward, and that "the wicked flee when no man pursueth."

At last he was seized by the flux, in Trichinopoly, where, as I mentioned, J. F. also died. He had been in the hospital a considerable time before I knew of his illness; and when I went up to see him, I observed that he was drawing very near his end. The agony he endured at that time was pressing the sweat through every pore of his body. Yet he was perfectly sensible; for when I spoke to him, he answered me in a very rational manner. But if the Lord be pleased to continue to me my reason and memory, until I also depart from this vale of tears, I think I will remember his last words until that hour.—After conversing a little with him, and when about to take my leave, I said to him, if it was the will of God that we should never again see one another in this world, I hoped we would meet in another and a better world. He answered me in the few following, but awfully important words, "*I know how I am, but I know not how I may be;*" taking (as good Mr. Boston expresses it) a leap in the dark, not knowing whether he should land in heaven or in hell. After making inquiry the next morning, I learned that his spirit returned to God who gave it about two hours after I left him. Having gone from our world, we cannot, we ought not, to follow him any farther; only this I will say, that he has received his sentence from him who can do him no wrong; for, "Shall not the Judge of all the earth do right?"

Now, from what we have seen of the life and death of these poor men, we may justly conclude that "the way of transgressors is hard." It was the saying of an old divine, that it required a person much harder labour to be damned than to be saved. We must acknowledge the idea to be just, although it may appear to be strangely expressed. But certain and true it is, that although these ways may seem right unto a man while he is walking in them, yet the end thereof is death. Now, although these persons whom I have just mentioned did not shoot themselves nor any of their comrades, yet the reader will easily perceive, by their conduct, the bad effects of evil principles and evil practices, which evidently led to the commission of such crimes as I have too justly charged upon some of the regiment.

CHAPTER VIII.

We left Masulipatam to proceed towards Madras, upon the 30th July, 1811, nothing taking place upon the march that I shall trouble you with. When we came to St. Thomas's Mount, (the place where the field force was formed,) it was expected that we were to take the duty of Fort St. George again; but, after being encamped, and in suspense for eight days, we were ordered to proceed to Trichinopoly.—This was a march of four weeks farther; so we left the Mount, and commenced our route towards that place upon the 17th of August, that day three years we left it, to take the field with the centre division of the army. I can hardly entertain you with any new thing upon our march, but an anecdote or two about the elephant. These useful animals, as I said before, carry the soldiers' tents upon the line of march, the oldest in the service generally taking the lead of the rest, carrying a white flag fastened to his load, the rest falling in quite naturally behind him: and I also stated that they follow the regiment or the army; and at no time, that ever I knew of, go before them. And I also, upon the field force, stated that the men frequently fall behind when the journey is very long; being unable many of them to sustain such fatigue. So one day, when we were hard travelled, a young lad who was scarcely able to draw the one foot past the other, (as we say,) was deliberating upon lying down upon the side of the road, and giving it up for a bad job, the leader of the elephants coming up with his white flag, before he was aware, (as they make no noise upon a sandy road,) quietly took the firelock from his shoulder, and gave it to the keeper, who was upon the neck of the animal, where they always ride, as upon a horse's back, carrying a small tomahawk, by which they direct him; but this is seldom needed, as they know every thing almost by the word of command. As I said, he took the firelock from the poor wearied soldier, and gave it to his keeper. The lad being much frightened, not knowing but the elephant intended knocking out his brains with it, gave a fearful stare, and ran off as quickly as his wearied limbs could carry him; but this alarm put fresh spirits into him, and perceiving that the benevolent animal meant him no harm but good, by easing him of his principal load; he came to the camp ground in company with his new acquaintance, whom he every now and then eyed with a look of uncertain satisfaction. I had this story from Serjeant Gray, who commanded the rear guard, a man whom I could believe as firmly as if I had witnessed the whole scene myself. But this is nothing very wonderful, in that truly wonderful animal; for the elephant attached to my own company and I got so very intimate upon the march, that he would not pass the tent of which I had charge, unless I came and spoke with him. Our friendship originated in this way; I used always to keep a piece of rice cake for him, when we could get it to ourselves for money; and while he was getting his morsel in the morning, the men of the tent would be packing the baggage on his back, and thereby we were generally first ready for the march, which was no small matter in our favour.

I could tell you many such stories, which I find more pleasure in, than telling you of men shooting themselves and one another; but these may serve as specimens. Although these creatures are possessed of most wonderful patience, as well as sagacity, yet they can be irritated, as I will make appear. I intend just to state one incident in proof of this, and then I have done with them. It is customary in this country to appoint a soldier of each European regiment to take care that the elephants are attended to upon the march, both with regard to work and provisions; and this person is generally a non-commissioned officer, who receives the appellation of elephant major. A serjeant who held this situation in the 30th regiment, one day loaded a poor fatigued animal with abuse, which he thought he was not at all entitled to. The elephant, observe you, did not immediately avenge himself of his adversary; but coolly waited his proper opportunity, and, in the course of the march, seeing his friend the serjeant at a distance, he embraced the moment when the water of a rice field was flowing across the road, filled his trunk with the sludge, and making up to the serjeant, who happened to have on a new suit of clothes, and of which he seemed to be very vain, he lodged the contents of his trunk upon the proud fellow's coat, and effectually spoiled its new gloss.

Upon this march, which, being in the rainy season, exposed us to constant wet, we crossed four rivers in boats; *viz.* two branches of the Kistna, and two branches of the Cauvery, which overflowed its banks at the time. We were obliged to lie by the side of the last mentioned river some days before we durst venture over, as the basket boats, formerly described, could not withstand such a current; but at last we got over with a considerable degree of difficulty and danger, though without any material damage. I had frequently, upon this march, taken up the resolution of the young man just mentioned, to give it up in despair; and had it not been for that kind of unconquerable spirit I seemed to be possessed of, I certainly would have made application for a doolie, which at this time was hardly to be obtained. I was, indeed, very near dying outright one day. The faithful companion of my toils, who used every means in her power for my benefit, prepared always (if possible) a draught for me when I came to the camp ground; but on this day it would not go down. She entertained very unfavourable hopes of me for some time, but, as the Lord would have it, after I rested a little, I was somewhat recruited; and being near the river last mentioned, we had a respite for a day or two, and being thereby something refreshed, I made out the march, which was four hundred and eighty-five miles, without the help of a doolie. The reader would not at all be surprised to hear of men dying, and giving up, upon a march in this country, if he could form a just idea of their hardships. On the very night before this, there was such a dreadful hurricane, that we could neither sit nor lie, but were obliged to stand and hold the poles of our tents, to keep the wind from carrying them away; and many of the tents were blown down, notwithstanding all the efforts of their inmates to support them; for the pins and cords were no security against the irresistible power of the airy element, but gave way like stubble before the sweeping blast. The ground, on which we had frequently to lie, was so deluged with the rain, that we were often up to the ancles in mud. All we could do in this case was to clear it away with a momatee, (a kind of scraper;) but, after all, the wet ground was a very unwholesome, uncomfortable bed. Our provisions, as I have mentioned before, were mutton and rice; and, had they been good, we would have had no just cause to complain; but, how could the sheep be in good condition in this country, when they live one half of the year upon the roots of grass, not a blade being to be seen during that time, except what grows by the sides of rivers or tanks? and marching them about with the army, you may be sure, did not at all improve their condition. I have looked at a chattie pot, (all their cooking utensils are made of earth, like our tiles or cans,) where half a sheep has been boiled, and, I assure you, there was not a vestige of fat to be seen: and then, the rice being cleaned and cooked in the open air, was always less or more mixed with sand. The only refreshing article we received was our two drams of liquor, which was a very acceptable beverage mixed with water; but I need not labour to make you enter into my feelings, for that would be impossible, unless you had experienced what I have done. However, I would not advise you to try the experiment to gratify your curiosity, or you may think it dear bought; and, in all probability, never come home to tell the tidings. I must say, indeed, that I was quite overjoyed when we received the route to go to India; but if I had known beforehand what I was to be subjected to in that country, I think, and not without cause, that I never would have been able to support the afflictions and hardships which fell to my lot; but the Lord, who is infinitely wise and merciful, in the exercise of that wisdom and mercy, has hid both the pains and pleasures of his dependent creatures from them, that "in the day of prosperity they may be moderately joyful, not knowing how soon afflictions may overtake them, and that in the day of adversity they may consider that the Lord may yet have many even temporal blessings in reserve for them; and by thus "setting the one over against the other," we may keep an equal, humble, and dependent mind; and thereby act under the injunction of the apostle, namely, to "weep as though we wept not, and rejoice as though we rejoiced not; and buy as though we possessed not; knowing that our time here is short, and that the fashion of this world passeth away."

We reached Trichinopoly upon the 5th October. This march, upon the whole, was the most severe I experienced in India, but it was the last I ever travelled upon foot. I was not long in Trichinopoly till I found the effects of my former troubles;

for I was seized with a liver complaint, and a general debility of the nervous system, which rendered me totally unfit for duty. I lingered long in this delicate state, and the doctor proposed sending me home, but the commanding officer was unwilling to part with me, still hoping that my disorder would take a favourable turn. My leading fifer was ordered to do my duty, and I had full liberty to walk about when able, wherever I pleased, and to amuse myself in any way I thought proper. In a word, I continued in this weakly state for about a twelvemonth, when it was found necessary that I should be invalided.

While we lay here, I received an addition to my family, in consequence of my wife having stood godmother for a child belonging to a serjeant of the regiment. But to enable you to understand the story properly, it will be needful to give you an outline of the mother's history, which I will do in as few words as possible.

Nelly Stevenson, (which was her maiden

name,) was the daughter of Wm. Stevenson, weaver in Anderston, Glasgow, with whom she lived until she was twenty years of age, at which time she was married to a young man of the name of M'Dougal, who volunteered into the Royals from the 26th regiment when in Dublin. This young man was one of the many who died of the flux when we lay in Wallajahbad. After his decease, she married a serjeant Fleming of the light company, by whom she had the child for whom my wife was sponsor; but this man lived with her only two years, when he also took the flux and died. In about six weeks afterwards *, she married a serjeant Lee of the grenadier company, by whom she had one child, and he being visited with the same disorder as her two former husbands, died also while we lay at Trichinopoly. She was now a widow the third time in the course of six years, and left

* The reader will naturally enough think it was a very strange thing of a woman to live so short time in widowhood; but if you consider the situation of

in a destitute state; but she did not need a fourth husband, because she was overtaken by the same fatal disorder that laid them in the dust, and died in about five weeks' illness, in the twenty-sixth year of her age. Now, in this case, it was plainly our duty to look after the child for which my wife stood, agreeably to the vows of God which were upon her; and a Serjeant Brown of the regiment, and his wife, took charge of Serjeant Lee's child, for whom they had become accountable, after the

these poor women, you perhaps may not be so much surprised at their apparently indelicate conduct; for they had no provision made for them whatever, except one pagoda per month, (eight shillings of our currency) allowed by the East India Company; and a reason fully as satisfactory as the former, was their unprotected state; for the barracks in this country are, in general, divided into two wings, without any partitions whatever. Now, just think of these women, without a guardian, day and night, in a room containing between four or five hundred men; and, alas! too many of them very immoral characters, to whose vile passions they presented a more tempting bait, from the scarcity of white women in the country.

manner of the Church of England. But I will say no more about this at present, as I will have occasion to speak of the last mentioned child again.

In the course of the time we lay in Trichinopoly, we had one Serjeant Clark affected with that dreadful disorder called hydrophobia, in rather a singular manner. This man being afflicted for some time with a very bad sore in his leg, and hearing that the tongue of a dog licking a sore of this kind had a very healing effect, he had recourse to this expedient, and coaxed a small dog in the barracks, which he took notice of sometimes, to do him, as he thought, this good office; but it would appear by the consequences that followed, that the dog had been disordered before it left off this practice, and before the serjeant was taken to hospital. It may seem strange to the reader, that this dog licking a sore, should produce so alarming an effect; but it was clearly proven, that the man himself had never been bitten; and there was a consultation of the faculty held upon this extraordinary case, who came to the conclusion, that the disease must have proceeded from this cause. The doctors tried repeatedly, and by various methods, to get him to swallow a little water, but all to no purpose; one of them attempted to give some to him in a concealed manner, putting it into what is called a hubble bubble, (a kind of pipe with a long tube, so that he could not see it); but whenever it came near him, he immediately took one of his shaking fits; and they were compelled to take it away without success.

Another extraordinary case of this extraordinary disease occurred while we lay in Masulipatam, which I shall just mention, and no more. One of the Company's artillery men, in the warm season, was seized with the disorder, but no person could tell how he came to be so affected, as there was no appearance of any bite about his body. This nonplussed the faculty completely, for they were sure enough that it was the hydrophobia; but how it had been produced they could not tell. Inquiry was made at his comrade, if he had known of his being bitten at any former period; and he told them, that he recollected perfectly of his being bitten about a twelvemonth ago; so, after they had deliberated for some time upon the accounts received, they came to the conclusion, that it was to the effects of this bite, though at such a distance of time, that he owed his death. Before I left the country, a kind of cure, it is said, was discovered for this most dreadful disorder. The cure seems quite natural; but as the way it was commonly said to have been discovered is strange, I shall give a very short account of it. One of the native women being bitten by a dog, and put into a place of confinement, contrived to make her escape, but when she was in the act of running away, some persons discovered her, and pursued her as fast as possible, and the poor creature, in her fright and trembling, fell all her length upon a place covered with broken bottles, and was no doubt cut and mangled dreadfully; however, the great quantity of blood that she lost was thought to have been the means of delivering her from this dreadful malady; and I understand that, since that time, bleeding a person almost to death, has repeatedly been tried with success in India, for this disease.

CHAPTER IX.

March 19, 1811.—We left Trichinopoly, to proceed to Bangalore. I had upon this march a doolie, for the first time since we came to India; and I had now travelled about 1600 miles with the Royals, since the regiment arrived in the country. We reached Bangalore upon the 12th of April; and, as I continued still very poorly, the doctor told the commanding officer, that it was in vain to keep me in India, in the hopes of regaining my health; for that was a thing not in the least to be expected, so I was ordered to be invalided. I accordingly passed the Board upon the 20th of August, along with thirty-two more;

but only eighteen of these were ordered for Europe.

I now, according to promise, resume my story of the little girl that went to Serjeant Brown at Trichinopoly, when we took home the orphan, to whom my wife had been godmother. This serjeant's wife was attacked by the flux, after we came to Bangalore, and being a woman grievously addicted to liquor, she was for some time abandoned by all the women who wished well to their character; but my wife hearing of her deplorable state, could not think of a countrywoman dying amongst black people, without any European woman paying the least attention to her. She determined, therefore, to render her what assistance was in her power; and, accordingly, went one day to her room, where she found her in a very loathsome state, attended only by her black female servant, and the child crying very much. She asked the woman what made the child cry so bitterly? to which she replied, *choar elia*, (that is, she has no meat; or rather, she is crying for hunger.) After putting clean clothes upon Mrs. Brown's bed, and doing all that she could do for her immediate comfort; she brought the poor starved little creature into our hut *, and said unto me, "O! Robert, if you will not take it amiss, I will keep this poor object, and see if I can do any thing for her." I cheerfully agreed to her humane proposal; and could scarcely help crying, when I saw the child crying; and my wife also bathed in tears. We accordingly kept the child, and Mrs. Brown still getting worse, died in a few days. My wife became much attached to the little girl; and the period drawing near when I had to leave the regiment, we proposed to Serjeant Brown to take her home to Scotland with us, but he formally refused, saying that he would get her brought up himself; but we could not think of leaving her in the country, as Serjeant Brown might soon be taken

* Some of the married people had liberty to build small houses for themselves outside the barracks.

from her by death *; and, likewise, because a man in his situation could not do his duty to a child like this, when he had no one but a black woman to look after his domestic matters; and besides, we could not think of taking her sister home, and leaving her in the country; so I spoke to the adjutant of the regiment, and it was soon settled that she was to accompany us.

This child was twenty months old when we took her home, and she could not set her foot upon the ground, more than if she had not been twenty weeks; she had the appearance of a monkey, more than any of the human species I ever saw; she was indeed nothing, I may say, but skin and bone; and was all covered over with a kind of white hairy down, and her skin, by being so much exposed to the sun with the black woman, was like a duck's foot, so that she was really a loathsome object; but by the time that she had been with us

* I have received word since I left the regiment of this man's death.

a few weeks, she not only could stand, but, to our great enjoyment, was able to walk about holding by my hand; but after she began to get a little flesh upon her, she broke all out into boils; many of them of such a size, as to require to be lanced by the doctor, and the scars of several of them remain upon her until this day; but I shall have occasion to speak about the children again; and, therefore, will say no more about them at present.

When I was upon the eve of leaving Bangalore, I thought if God spared me to return home, I might expect to see some of the friends and relatives of the men, who would be inquiring after them; I, therefore, wished to make myself acquainted as well as possible with the state of the regiment; and, for this purpose went to the orderly room, and received a statement of the men who had died and gone home invalids; I shall merely mention the number, as the names would be of no use to the reader. Total strength of his Majesty's 1st, or Royal Scots, after the grenadier company joined in Wallajahbad, 1006. Joined at different periods since the regiment came to India, 941; that is, a total of 1947 men, out of which number have died, and been invalided unfit for further service, eight hundred and forty-five.— Number of women that came to the country with the regiment, sixty-two; joined at different periods, twenty, out of which died thirty-two. We had at this time only two children in life that came out with the regiment, and the total number of children that died upon the passage, and since we landed, fifty-seven; that is a total of nine hundred and thirty-four, including invalids, in less than seven years. There were also eight women who left their husbands in the country, and went to officers of different regiments, being "drawn away of their own lust and enticed;" that insatiable desire of "wearing of gold and putting on of apparel," displayed by too many, was their ruin; but before I left the country, three of these poor wretches died in great misery, and four of them became common prostitutes about Madras. The remaining female of this unhappy class, in consequence of some disease, was reduced to such a state of decrepitude, as to be drawn about in a small cart, being unable to walk. What a pity, and a shame it is, that ever such scenes should be exhibited by those who bear the name of Christians; and, particularly, in a country which we are labouring to Christianize. Sure I am, that it operates greatly against the success of these excellent missionaries, whose labours are carried on near any of our regiments; for, when the natives see the shamefully inconsistent conduct of the soldiers and other Europeans, they cannot but think that their own religion is better than that of our countrymen, since, generally speaking, these are much inferior to them in point of sobriety, and some other moral habits.

It is easier for the Christian reader to

conceive, than for me to describe, my feelings for a few days previous to leaving the regiment; but just place yourself, as it were, in my circumstances, and let the past and the future be present to your mind : suppose yourself to have been for seven years absent from your native country, and from all those who were near and dear to you at home, and, above all, from the public ordinances of divine grace, and to have been travelling in that wilderness wherein (both literally and figuratively) there was often no way; and also to have been as it were at the gates of death, when there could be little rational hope entertained of ever being brought up again, much less of having the joyful anticipation of soon being restored to your native country, your friends, and even perhaps to a health of which you had long been deprived ; and, in a word, to pure air, pure water, and, above all, to a pure Gospel—I say, suppose yourself placed in these circumstances, and see if you will wonder when I tell you my joyful feelings were excited almost to rapture upon this occasion. But you may be ready to say, was there nothing I was leaving behind me calculated to raise in my mind feelings of an opposite kind? No affectionate friends with whom I had enjoyed agreeable fellowship? No doubt there were such friends, and I bless God I can say, that they were friends who had not only travelled part of the weary way with me in that wilderness, but whose society I hope to enjoy again in the promised land; and when I saw and thought on such friends, my mind was no doubt agitated, and a conflict of joy and grief was awakened in my breast. I will just select one solitary individual for my present purpose, as her situation was peculiarly trying, and consequently better calculated to touch the sympathetic feelings, by way of illustrating what I have stated; namely, that I was not without friends from whose social and religious fellowship I was about to be separated.

This person was a young woman, named Mrs. Copwick, who came along with her husband from his Majesty's 33d, when the volunteers from that regiment joined us before they embarked for Europe. Her father and mother had been for a number of years in the regiment, and she was born and brought up in it; and when she attained her 18th year, the old people encouraged her to keep company with the drill serjeant of the corps, who was a man of very depraved habits, and who, in point of years, might have been her father, but he knew how to manage their failings by his own experience, and used to give them many a hearty treat of liquor for her sake, and to gratify his own insatiable desire for drinking at the same time.

The consequence was, notwithstanding the poor girl's disinclination, that her parents got them joined together in a marriage contract. Mrs. C. had been in our regiment for some time before I was acquainted with her, and our acquaintance arose from my wife bringing her into our hut shortly after we came to Bangalore. We were several times in each other's company before we had any conversation of a religious kind; and the first time that I may say any of us had a favourable opportunity was, I think, one Sabbath forenoon, when I was engaged reading Doddridge's Rise and Progress. I happened to make some observations on the subject, which gave her a suitable opportunity of opening her mind to me, which, it struck me, from some previous circumstances, she had been desirous of doing. I was truly delighted with the simple, undisguised manner in which she expressed her sentiments and feelings, and happy that I had it partly in my power to relieve the uneasiness of her mind, and to assist her inquiries after divine truth. From this time we endeavoured to make it convenient frequently to have some discourse together in our hut; the Sabbath, in a particular manner, being devoted by us for our mutual edification; and she found it a very severe trial indeed to be compelled to exchange our company and conversation for the company and unprofitable conversation of the men, when she went to her barrack-room at night, and, above all, to face her brutal husband, who perceived by her artless manner of endeavouring to persuade him to leave off his wicked courses, how she had been employed. Her attempts to reclaim him, alas! were all in vain, for the best answer that she would receive from him for this kindest of all love, was to keep her tongue to herself, and not trouble him with her —— nonsense; and if she attempted, while he was defaming, to entreat, it was well if he did not enforce his denunciations by the weight of an unmerciful hand. Such was the miserable situation of this poor female, who had, besides this, the care of two young children, and was unwearied in her endeavours to make her husband and them comfortable. Now, my dear reader, if you have been placing yourself all along in my circumstances, you will certainly partake, in part, of my feelings; but, after all, it will only be in part; for although the power of imagination is great, yet I am persuaded you will come far short of the reality; still I am sure you will not wonder at my being sorry to part with this truly amiable young woman, who was earnestly desirous to obtain the knowledge of that way in which she might "escape the wrath to come," and in whom I felt the more deeply interested from a consideration of my former situation in the Prince of Wales's Island, where I so earnestly desired some person to assist me in inquiries of a similar kind. Now, all that I could do for her in this case, (for parted we must be,) was to give her my advice, my best gift*, and my blessing with it,

* She had already a Bible of her own.

namely, Doddridge's Rise and Progress of Religion in the Soul, (which book I formerly mentioned having purchased from one of the men in Hydrabad,) and which had been of great use to myself; and I hope the blessing of God has rendered it of great service to her also. In a word, we parted with very sorrowful hearts, but our sorrow was not without hope, for that blessed religion which had formerly supported our minds, and cheered us in many a gloomy hour, left us not even now, when we needed comfort; but told us that the sufferings of the present time were not worthy to be compared with the glory that should be revealed in us at our meeting in Emmanuel's land; and that our light afflictions which might intervene, were but for a moment, and would, by the divine blessing, work out for us a far more exceeding and eternal weight of glory.

The invalids left Bangalore upon the 13th September, 1813, and proceeded to Punamalee, a depôt for recruits from Europe, and invalids from India, homeward bound. We were ordered there to be in readiness for the first Company's ship that should touch at Madras. We arrived at Punamalee upon the 1st of October, 1813. I had in this place a severe attack of the bile upon the stomach; but it was not the disorder generally called by that name in this country; for it has nearly all the symptoms of the flux, being accompanied with great pain in the bowels, which are generally much swelled, along with a considerable degree of sickness. I was so much exhausted by it in two days, that I could not turn myself in the bed without assistance. I continued about a week very ill, and had more the appearance of getting a grave in India, than of ever seeing my native country again; but it was the wise saying of a worthy divine, that man is immortal until his day come; for while there are more days, there are means stirred up. But often, since I came to India, have I been inclined to take up the language of good

Hezekiah, " I have said in the cutting off of my days, I shall go to the gates of the grave; I am deprived of the residue of my years. I said I shall not see the Lord, even the Lord, in the land of the living; I shall behold man no more with the inhabitants of the world." But I can now add, with the same good man, " O Lord, thou hast in love to my soul delivered it from the pit of corruption; thou hast cast all my sins behind thy back: for the grave cannot praise thee; death cannot celebrate thee; they that go down to the pit cannot hope for thy truth: the living, the living, he shall praise thee, as I do this day." O that I may devote my spared life unto thy service.

While we lay at Punamalee, Paddy L—, of our regiment, drowned himself in a tank, at the back of the barracks, upon a Sabbath morning. This man was going along ith us for Europe, with a bad discharge, in consequence of having made himself unfit for further service by shooting off his hand, for which dreadful outrage against the laws of both God and man, as well as against his own body, he was sentenced to receive corporal punishment; to be kept in confinement during his stay with the regiment; and to be sent home with a blank discharge. He had also been frequently confined, after we came here, for different crimes; and once while he was in the *Cungie-house*,* having obtained a light, on pretence of lighting his pipe, he set fire to the place, attempting to burn both it and himself; and it was with considerable difficulty that his life, at that time, was saved, being taken out half suffocated, and as black as a chimney-sweep. I cannot inform the reader what were his diabolical motives for drowning himself;

* The *Cungie-house* is intended to answer the same purpose as the black-hole for soldiers in this country; where the prisoners receive for subsistence boiled rice, and the water with which it is made ready, which kind of food is called *Cungie*; and from which also the place above mentioned receives the appellation *Cungie-house*.

but we need not wonder much at it, when he was so depraved as to commit such crimes as I have mentioned, and indeed many others which I decline noticing; only this I will say, that "destruction and misery are in the way of such people, and the way of peace they have not known;" and no marvel that "their feet run into evil, and make haste to shed blood, seeing they have no fear of God before their eyes."

While here also I received a letter from Serjeant Gray, giving us the melancholy intelligence of his wife having had a severe attack of the flux, and of that disorder terminating in her dissolution, and earnestly soliciting me to send him a word of consolation, and an advice suited to the particularly trying circumstances in which he was placed; to which request I most readily complied in the best way I was able. My wife and I were much affected at the unexpected news; and no wonder, considering that great intimacy which had always subsisted between our families ever since the time I received Doddridge's Rise and Progress in Hydrabad. Our attachment to one another was such, that during the time the regiment was in Trichinopoly, when our huts were at a considerable distance, we very seldom passed a day, if duty would permit, without being in one another's company, and frequently we even dined together; and this friendship subsisted until we left the regiment, when we had truly a sorrowful parting; but we then little imagined that one of us was so near the eternal world. Surely the language of Divine Providence to us at this time was, "Be ye also ready, for at such an hour as ye think not the Son of Man cometh." Surely this is an important, universal, and perpetual admonition, "O that we were wise, that we understood this, that we would consider our latter end." My letter no sooner reached the regiment, than Mrs. Copwick seeing it, wrote off immediately to Punamalee, requesting me very kindly "to send her also a word of advice before our embarkation; adding, that although she had not forgotten my former counsels, yet she had a great desire to have something from me in writing, that would not only refresh her memory, but also excite her gratitude to her heavenly Father, who had used me as an instrument, that Christ might be formed in her soul, and that it might also be a help to support her mind, under her severe trials, and encourage her to a continuance in well-doing, trusting that at last she might receive the end of her faith, even the salvation of her soul."

I need scarcely inform the Christian reader with what joy I received this delightful letter, and with what comfort and enlargement of heart I answered it; all that I shall say is, that I wish God may bless every mean which I have been enabled to use for her eternal advantage, and that we may finally meet again upon the right hand of the judge, when he which soweth, and they which reap, shall rejoice together.

I have since learned from good authority, that Serjeant Gray has followed his wife to the narrow house appointed for all living, and that Mrs. C.'s wicked husband is also gone from our world, dying as he had lived, and that God, in his kind providence, has provided a friend who took an interest in the welfare of his widow, and obtained a place for her in the family of a respectable clergyman in the country, to take the superintendence of his children, having made ample provision both for her and the orphans. In their happy experience, therefore, was that promise fulfilled*, "Leave thy fatherless children, I will preserve them alive, and let your widows trust in me."

My dear reader, you may naturally enough think that the writer of this little work is very defective in his duty, when he has travelled so many hun-

* Only, to be sure, in a certain sense; but it would have been verified strictly if the serjeant had been one of God's people.

dred miles in India, and has scarcely so much as even dropped a hint of the appearance of the country, the customs and manners of its inhabitants, their religion, &c.; but my reason for this is, that I may make this work appear as regular and satisfactory as possible; for I have designedly delayed entering upon these things until I was just going to take farewell of the country. And now, as I am going to take a long, and, I hope, a last adieu of that part of the world, where I have suffered much, and, I bless God, have enjoyed much, I will attempt a very brief account of these, in their regular order, before I step on board ship, and close my bodily eyes—for ever perhaps—upon this scene.

CHAP. X.

Country.—I do not mean here to give you a particular description of the various parts of India through which I have travelled, but rather attempt a very brief sort of general representation of it: and I will say that it is, comparatively, sandy and barren; for water, which is so essential to the fertilizing of the soil, is in most places very scarce; and no wonder, when it is generally six or seven months in the year without a shower of rain. And were it not for a plan adopted by the natives, where there are no rivers, by far the greater part of the country, now peopled, would be uninhabitable; but during the monsoon, or rainy season, the inhabitants, having prepared large tanks for its reception, get these amply stored during the heavy rains; which I have often seen fall in such abundance as to inundate the country so that the communication betwixt villages, (which are always built upon rising ground,) had to be carried on by boats or canoes. I say, when these tanks are filled, it secures to them, humanly speaking, the succeeding harvest. The event is celebrated with great rejoicings; but I shall not waste your time and my own, in attempting to describe these ostentatious parades, but desire rather that you would turn over your Bible, and look at Belshazzar's mob of musicians, described in the 3d chapter of Daniel, for you will there find the description of a similar band; and it is very easy to conceive, in your own mind, a number of black people following them. I will rather give you a sketch of the manner in which their crops are produced, which will be more entertaining and instructive.

After, therefore, having these tanks well replenished, and before they begin to plough their rice-fields*, (which must be always nearly level,) they flood them with water for a day or two, to soften the ground; and, to effect this, they have recourse to the following expedient: they erect a thick post about twelve feet high, at the top of which there is a strong lever, somewhat like the handle of our pump wells, only much longer, and to that end to which you may suppose the sucker of the pump attached, they fasten a rope or chain, of a sufficient length to reach the water, and, at the end of this rope or chain, they have a large iron bucket, and a person ready, at the side of the tank, to guide and empty it into the furrows or ridges, (Psalm lxv. 9th verse and downward,) which are formed in the rice-fields for

* Rice, in this country, may be called the staff of life.

the reception of the water, and also to conduct it over the surface of the whole plain that they intend to water. At the other end of the lever another person is appointed to tread on it, so as to raise up or let down the bucket to the person, as I said, who stands at the bottom to guide and empty it; and, to prevent the feet of the drawer from slipping, there are a number of knobs or blocks of wood nailed upon that part of the handle which he treads. These water-engines are frequently erected by the side of a growing tree; but when this is not to be had, there are two large uprights placed close by the supposed pump, and spaked across, so that the person may not only ascend and descend upon this kind of ladder, but also have a security from falling, while he is following his employment. This is the mode of watering fields, I may say, universally adopted in India, where I have travelled; but there is another kind of water-engine, which I understand is generally used in Egypt, and some other countries, which is managed by the motion of a wheel. In this wheel there are a number of steps, and the person treading upon these turns the wheel round until the rope or chain has elevated the bucket to a level with the soil intended to be watered; but whether the one or the other plan be adopted, it is a laborious and scanty manner of watering cultivated grounds of any extent. If the inhabitants of these parched countries were obliged to adopt this mode for their gardens only, it would be comparatively trifling labour; but when a person takes a view of a very extensive field, which must be kept two or three inches deep all the time the rice is growing, (and only when they wish the rice to harden is it taken off,) I say, if we consider this, the reasoning of the inspired historian, in showing the superiority of the land of Canaan to that of Egypt, will be very evident.

Deuteronomy xi. 10. " For the land whither thou goest to possess it, is not like the land of Egypt, from whence ye came out, where thou sowedst thy seed, and wateredst it with thy foot, as a garden of herbs: but the land whither ye go to possess it, is a land of hills and valleys, and drinketh water of the rain of heaven; a land which the Lord thy God careth for: the eyes of the Lord thy God are always upon it, from the beginning of the year even to the end of the year."

Although I have said that the country is comparatively sandy and barren, yet I say, that many parts of it also, which are situated on the banks of rivers, are very fertile. The finest parts of India that I have seen are near the Kisna and Tamboothera; these rivers supplying their neighbourhood abundantly, give it a very fresh and delightful appearance; and, O! how it cheers the spirits, and invigorates the eye of the " wayfaring man," to come into the view of a considerable tract of country, covered with woods and various kinds of herbage, after having travelled days, or even weeks, and scarcely ever seen any object to relieve the fatigued eye; but, on the contrary, every thing to offend and hurt it; nothing presenting itself on any side but glistening sand, scraggy bushes, the shining arms of the soldiery, and the dazzling exhalations of the morning dews. Surely, "Blessed is the man that trusteth in the Lord, and whose hope the Lord is: for he shall be as a tree, planted by the waters, and that spreadeth out her roots by the river, and shall not see when heat cometh; but her leaf shall be green, and shall not be careful in the year of drought, neither shall cease from yielding fruit." The analogy of this figure is simple and beautiful, and the application natural and easy, from what I have been stating, to the pious and reflective mind.

Manners, Customs, &c.—The complexion of the Hindoos is black; their hair is long; their persons in general are straight and well-formed, and their countenances open and pleasant. The dress of the men amongst the higher ranks is a white vest of silk, muslin, or cotton, girt with a sash; the sleeves are very long; and the upper part of the garment contrived to fit, so that the wearer's shape may be seen; their trowsers descend so low as to cover their legs; they wear slippers down in the heel, and peaked at the toes, into which they put their naked feet. The dress of the women amongst the higher or middle ranks, is a piece of white calico tied about the waist, which reaches to their knees; and the vest is thrown across their shoulders, covering the breasts and part of the back; their hair, like that of the men, is tied up in a roll, and adorned with jewels, or toys; they wear pendants in their ears, and several strings of beads round their necks; they also wear rings upon their fingers and toes, and bracelets upon their wrists and ankles.

The Hindoos are, in general, very sober, and abstain from all animal food. The Brahmins, in particular, never eat any thing that has had the breath of life: *curees* of vegetables are their common diet; the chief ingredients of which are turmeric, spices, and the pulp of the cocoa-nut. They esteem milk the purest food; and venerate the cow almost as a divinity.

In manners, they are effeminate, luxurious, and taught to affect a grave deportment. This initiates them early in the arts of dissimulation; so that they can caress those whom they hate, and even behave with kindness to those whom they intend to murder*. The common saluta-

* We had several of our regiment who attached themselves to black women, by whom they were poisoned; one, in particular, suffered under a long lingering illness. This young man was the Paymaster's clerk, who had taken one of these women (who had broken her caste) and kept her for a considerable time, but, happening to have some words with her one day, he threatened to put her away; and she, taking it for granted that he would be as good as his

tion is, by lifting one or both hands to the head, according to the quality of the person saluted; but no person salutes with the left hand singly.

On visiting amongst friends, the master of the house never rises to receive his visitor, but requests him to come and sit down beside him on the carpet or floor; and the betle-nut-box is presented to him, as we do our snuff-boxes. This betle-nut is used in the same manner as we do tobacco; and both the men and the women take it indiscriminately.

Dancing girls are generally engaged at public entertainments to amuse the company. They adorn their necks with carcanets, their arms with bracelets, and their ankles with small gold or silver chains.

word, gave him a dose of poison; but afterwards lived with him for some time, with all the apparent affection that a wife should show for a husband; nor did she leave him until a suspicion arose that she was the person who had done the wicked deed. This young man died; and his body having been opened by the surgeon, he was found to have been poisoned.

The dance of these women is a cadenced movement, performed to the sound of a drum, (called a tum-tum,) which a person beats upon with his fingers, and accompanies with a song, that, to a person possessed of any taste, is truly barbarous. The mode of beating time is with a small bell, or cymbal, which the dancing-master holds in his hand. This bell, or cymbal, he beats against the edge of another of the same kind, which produces a brisk vibrating sound, which animates the dancers, and gives precision to their movements. They, however, display no elegant attitudes, but are full of gesture; and the motion of their arms seems to occupy their whole attention.

The manner of drinking among the Hindoos is remarkable. They religiously avoid touching the vessel with their lips, but pour it into their mouths, holding the vessel at a distance. Their notion is, that they would be polluted by drinking any stagnant liquid. Thus, they will drink from a pump, or any clear running stream, but not out of a standing pool. On a march, when any of the natives made their appearance with their jimbos, (a small vessel, generally of brass or earth,) we were driven by thirst sometimes to leave the ranks, and entreated them to permit us to drink; but it was always in vain; and if any of us took the vessel by force into our hands, either to swallow its contents, or to draw water for ourselves, they broke it to pieces, and raised the hue and cry that they were polluted and ruined; and any soldier so acting would expose himself to a severe flogging. But I have known some instances, wherein some of those people, possessed of more generous minds and liberal sentiments, have given us to drink, when we held our hands at each side of our mouth, while they poured the water into them, holding the jimbo about half a yard above our head; but, in this case, we were more satisfied externally than internally.

The houses in Hindostan are for the most part very mean; in front of these houses are sheds on pillars, under which the natives expose their goods for sale, and entertain their friends. No windows open towards the streets, and even the palaces of their princes have not any external elegance. The marriages of the wealthy Hindoos are conducted with the utmost splendour and extravagance. The little bride and bridegroom, who are frequently only three or four years of age, are for several nights carried through the streets, richly dressed, and adorned with the finest jewels their parents can procure, preceded by flags, music, and a multitude of lights. The astrologer having fixed on a fortunate hour, they are taken to the house of the bride's father, and being seated opposite to each other, with a table between them, they join their hands across it, and the priest covers both their heads with a kind of hood, which remains spread over them about a quarter of an hour, while he prays for their happiness, and gives them the nuptial benediction; after which, their heads are uncovered, and all the company are sprinkled with perfumes, and the evening concludes with a magnificent entertainment for the friends who attend.

The Hindoo women, in general, treat their husbands with great respect; and very few are ever known to violate the marriage bed. They begin to bear children at twelve years of age, and sometimes younger; but they seldom have any after they are thirty; and frequently before that time they lose their bloom, and begin to fade. With respect to the funerals of the Hindoos, some of them bury the body, and others burn it. The ceremony of burning is performed in the following manner:—Having washed and dressed the corpse, the relations and friends carry it on a bier to a small distance from the town. This is usually done the next day; but if a person die in the morning, his body is always burnt the same evening; for, in this country, a corpse will not keep long. The funeral pile is usually made near some river or tank; and if he be a person of rank, great quantities of fragrant wood are mixed with the fuel. As soon as the corpse is placed upon the pile, and some prayers muttered by the attending Brahmin, the fire is applied at one of the corners, when it soon blazes up, and consumes the body to ashes.

The horrid practice of widows burning themselves along with the corpse of their deceased husbands is losing ground very fast in India; and there is scarcely ever an instance of it now known in our settlements; and, as far as I could learn, when performed at all, it is chiefly confined to the Brahmin cast.

Religion, &c.—The religion of the Hindoos is all contained in the sacred books called Vedas. These books are supposed to have been the work, not of the supreme God himself, but of an inferior deity called Brimha. They inform us that Brahma, the supreme god, having created the world by the word of his mouth, formed a female deity, named Bawaney, who brought forth three male deities, named Brimha, Vishnu, and Seeva. They say that Brimha was endowed with the power of creating all things, Vishnu with that of cherishing them, and Seeva the power of restraining them. They say also, that Brahma himself endowed mankind with passions and understanding to regulate them; while Brimha created the inferior beings, and afterwards employed himself in writing the Vedas, and gave these to the Brahmins to be explained. These Brahmins are allowed to be the most honourable tribe amongst the Hindoos, and are alone appointed to officiate in the priesthood, like the Levites among the Jews. They alone are allowed to read the Vedas or sacred books; and to them are committed the instruction of the people. There are several orders of these Brahmins: those who mix in society are not unfrequently of depraved morals; and we need not wonder that it should be the case, when they are taught by their religion that the water of the Ganges will effectually wash away all their sins. Those Brahmins who live secluded from society, are men of very weak minds, or enthusiasts, who give themselves up to indolence and superstition. The Chehteree, or second caste, is next in rank to the Brahmins; and from this caste their Nabobs, or Princes, are always chosen.

The Bice, or Banians, who compose the third class, are those people whose profession is trade and merchandise. They have no particular religion, unless it be adherence to truth in their words and dealings. They are the great factors by whom the trade of India is carried on; and, as they believe in the transmigration of souls, they eat no living creature, nor kill even noxious animals, but endeavour to release them from the hands of others who may be intending to destroy them.

I have seen them feeding the mice and bandicauts with grain or rice in the bazaar.

The Soodera, or fourth class, is the most numerous, and comprehends all labourers and artists. These are divided into as many orders as there are followers of different arts; all the children being invariably brought up to the profession of their forefathers.

The temples of the Hindoos (called by them pagodas) are large, but disgusting stone buildings, erected in every capital, and are under the direction of the Brahmins. The pagoda of Seringham, near the place where we crossed the Cavery, and which we passed on our way to Trichinopoly, is allowed to be the most stupendous, and is held the most sacred of any building of the kind in India, that of Chillambraum excepted. This pagoda is situated about a mile from the western extremity of the island of Seringham, formed by the division of the great river Cavery into two channels. It is composed of seven square inclosures, one within the other, the walls of which are twenty-five feet high, and four thick. These inclosures have each four large gates: the outer wall which surrounds this pagoda is between three and four miles in circumference, and its gateway to the south is ornamented with pillars, several of which are single stones, thirty-three feet long, and about four in diameter. The walls of this building is covered outside with the most hideous figures, likenesses of which are to be found neither "in heaven above, nor on the earth beneath, nor in the waters under the earth;" so that persons would not literally be guilty of a breach of the second command if they were to fall down and worship them,—such as men with elephants' heads, serpents with men's heads, bullocks with women's head and breasts, &c. and monsters which I have never before nor since seen or heard off, and these painted in the most glaring colours. Here also, as in the other great pagodas of India, the

Brahmins live without subordination, and slumber in a voluptuousness which knows no wants. This pagoda is about four miles from Trichinopoly.

There are several sects among the Hindoos, but their differences consist rather in external forms than religious opinions. They all believe in the immortality of the soul; a state of future rewards and punishments; and transmigration of souls. The virtues of charity and hospitality exist amongst them, both in theory and practice, towards those of their own caste. They say that hospitality is commanded to be exercised even towards an enemy; and they use this simile, "the tree doth not withdraw its shade from the wood-cutter, or water-drawer, nor doth the moon withhold her light from the chandalah." These pure doctrines, however, are intermixed with many vile superstitions. The Hindoos pray thrice in the day, at morning, noon, and evening, turning their faces towards the east. Fruits, flowers, incense, and money, are the usual offerings to their idols; but, for the dead, they offer a particular sort of cake called punda. They all seem to pay an extraordinary veneration to fire, and always wash before meals.

There is a religious order among the Hindoos, called Fakirs: these are a kind of begging friars, who make vows of poverty, and seem insensible both to pleasure and pain. They generally live upon the bounty of the smaller kind of merchants; and I have seen them often carrying a small copper jimbo, (vessel,) in the form of a water-melon, when they were begging through the bazaars. These Fakirs, to obtain the favour of Brahma as they suppose, suffer the most dreadful tortures; and the austerities which some of them undergo are incredible to those who have not been eye-witnesses of them: some of them stand for months upon one foot, with their arms tied to the beam of a house, by which means their arms settle in that posture, and ever after become useless;

some sit in the sun, with their faces looking upwards, until they are incapable of altering the position of their heads; and I even saw one in Bangalore, who had a large sort of iron grating fixed upon his neck, that had not stretched himself upon a bed, or even upon the ground, for two years. But the people, in all these cases, deem it an act of piety to encourage and support them.

The ordeal trials of melted lead, or boiling oil, as practised in India, are considered by the Hindoos as a standing miracle. The ceremony, which is in the following manner, is performed with great solemnity: The party who has appealed to this form of trial for his innocence, whether on suspicion of murder, theft, or unfaithfulness to the marriage bed on the part of women, is publicly brought to the side of a fire, on which is placed a vessel of boiling water or oil, but most commonly melted lead; the magistrates of the country or city being present, his hand is washed clean, and the leaf of a particular tree, with his accusation written upon it, is tied about his waist; and then, on a solemn invocation of the deity by the Brahmin, the person plunges in his hand and scoops up the boiling fluid! and if he draws it out unhurt, he is absolved; but if otherwise, he receives the punishment due to the crime charged against him.

The ceremonies of the Hindoos are dictated by the Brahmins and the sacred books; but to give you a detail of their number and absurdity, is a task to which I am altogether unequal, and which could neither instruct nor entertain the reader. I will, therefore, close this sketch with giving you a few translations from their Vedas or sacred books, which will give the reader some idea both of the doctrines and style of the Hindoos, as translated by a very able pen.

"1. By one Supreme Ruler is this universe pervaded, even every world in the whole circle of nature; enjoy pure delights,

O man! by abandoning all thoughts of this perishable world; and covet not the wealth of any creature existing.

"2. He who in this life continually performs his religious duties, may desire to live a hundred years; but, even to the end of this period, thou shouldst have no other employment here below.

"3. To those regions where evil spirits dwell, and which utter darkness involve, all such men go surely after death, as destroy the purity of their own souls.

"4. There is one supreme Spirit, which nothing can shake, more swift than the thought of man.

"5. That supreme Spirit moves at pleasure, but in itself is immovable; it is distant from us, yet very near us; it pervades this whole system of worlds, yet is infinitely beyond it.

"6. The man who considers all beings as existing even in the supreme Spirits, and the supreme Spirit pervading all beings, henceforth views no creature with contempt.

"7. In him who knows that all spiritual beings are the same in kind with the Supreme Spirit, what room can there be for delusion of mind; or what room for sorrow, when he reflects on the identity of spirit?

"8. The pure enlightened soul assumes a luminous form, with no gross body, with no perforation, with no veins nor tendons, untainted by sin, itself being a ray from the infinite Spirit, which knows the past and the future, which pervades all, which existed with no cause but itself, which created all things as they are in ages very remote.

"9. They who are ignorantly devoted to the mere ceremonies of religion, are fallen into thick darkness; but they surely have a thicker gloom around them who are solely given to speculation.

"10. A distinct reward, they say, is reserved for ceremonies, and a distinct reward, they say, for divine knowledge; adding, this we have heard from sages who declared it unto us.

"11. He alone is acquainted with the nature of ceremonies, and with that of speculative science, who is acquainted with both at once; by religious ceremonies he passes the gulf of death, and, by divine knowledge he attains immortality.

"12. They who adore only the appearances and forms of the Deity, are fallen into thick darkness; but they surely have a thicker gloom around them, who are solely devoted to the abstract existence of the divine essence.

"13. A distinct reward, they say, is obtained by adoring the forms and attributes; and a distinct reward, they say, by adoring the abstract essence; adding, this we have heard from sages who declared it to us.

"14. He only knows the forms and essence of the Deity who adores both at once; by adoring the appearance of the Deity, he passes the gulf of death; and by adoring his abstract essence, he attains immortality.

"15. Unvail, O thou who givest sustenance to the world, the face of the true sun, which is now hidden by a vase of golden light! so that we may love the truth, and know our whole duty.

"16. O thou, who givest sustenance to the world; thou sole mover of all; thou who restrainest sinners; who pervadest yon great luminary; who appearest as the sun of the creator, hide thy dazzling beams, and expand thy spiritual brightness, that I may view thy most glorious, real form!"

The following is translated from a Sanscrit work, entitled, "The Ignorant Instructed."

"1. Restrain, O ignorant man, thy desire of wealth, and become a hater of it in body, understanding, and mind; let the riches thou possessest be acquired by thy own good actions: with this gratify thy soul.

"2. The boy so long delights in his play; the youth so long pursues his beloved; the old so long broods over melancholy thoughts, that no man meditates on the supreme Being.

"3. Who is thy wife, and who is thy son? How great and wonderful is this world! Whose thou art, and whence thou comest? Meditate on this, my brother; and again on this.

"4. Be not proud of wealth, and thy attendants, and youth; since time destroys them all, in the twinkling of an eye: check thy attachment to all these illusions, like Moyra; fix thy heart on the foot of Brahma, and thou wilt soon know him.

"5. As a drop of water on the leaf of the lotus, thus, or more slippery, is human life: the company of the virtuous endures here but for a moment; that is the vehicle to bear thee over land and ocean.

"6. To dwell in the mansions of God, at

the foot of a tree; to have the ground for a bed, and a hide for a vesture; to renounce all ties of family or connections: who would not receive delight from this abhorrence of the world?

"7. Set not thy affections on foe or friend; on a son or a relation; in war or in peace, bear an equal mind towards all: if thou desiredst it, thou wilt soon be like Vishnu.

"8. Day and night, evening and morn, winter and spring, depart and return: time sports, age passes on; desire and the wind continue unrestrained.

"9. When the body is tottering, the head grey, and the mouth toothless; when the smooth stick trembles in the hand it supports, yet the vessel of covetousness is unemptied.

"10. So soon born, so soon dead; so long lying in thy mother's womb, so great crimes are committed in the world. How then, O man! canst thou live here below with complacency?

"11. There are eight original mountains,

and seven seas:—Brahma, Indra, the Sun, and Kudra,—these are permanent; not thou, not I, not this or that people; what, therefore, should occasion our sorrow?

"12. In thee, in me, in every other, Vishnu resides; in vain art thou angry with me, not bearing my reproach: this is perfectly true, all must be esteemed equal; be not proud of a magnificent palace."

When the reader takes a cursory view of the principal doctrines and precepts of the Hindoo Vedas, he may be very apt to imagine that the writer, or writers, have received their information from some other source than the fragments of a broken law, which are still imprinted upon the mind of man, even in a state of nature; and he may not unlikely suppose, that these men had this knowledge—although remote and much corrupted, from our sacred volume; particularly as that part, entitled "The Ignorant Instructed," seems to partake of the style of Solomon in the book of Ecclesiastes. But if you make a more minute investigation, you will see much wanting, and much wrong; and no marvel, for they who are deprived of the great blessing of revelation, or they who despise it, or wish to be wise above what is written, are like people groping in the dark; and will certainly either fall short of the truth, or stumble over it altogether. Those sages of antiquity, to whom the writers seem to refer, were perhaps distinguished for their wisdom; yet by that very wisdom they knew not God in his saving characters. Man may know, to a certain extent, that there is a God; because "the heavens declare his glory, and the firmament sheweth his handy-works." And the apostle says, in his epistle to the Romans, that "the Gentiles, which have not the law, do by nature the things contained in the law, these, having not the law, are a law unto themselves: which shew the work of the law written in their hearts; their conscience also bearing witness, and their thoughts the meanwhile accusing, or else excusing one another." I say, therefore, that by the external and internal aid which man is possessed of, even in a state of nature, he may know by natural religion that there is a God; yet it is impossible that he should come to the knowledge of God in reference to man, as a guilty, depraved, miserable captive, and yet a condemned slave, redeemed by a price of infinite value. No; it never has, it never will, "enter into the heart of man," unassisted by revelation, to come to a saving knowledge of God, "even that knowledge which is eternal life." Let us, therefore, bless God for our Bibles, and willingly give our prayers, and our purses also, "according as God hath prospered us," to send the Gospel to that country "where there is no vision, and where the people are perishing for lack of this knowledge;" for, "How can they believe in him of whom they have not heard? and how can they hear without preachers? and how can they preach except they be sent?" And, when we consider that there are computed to be no less than sixty millions even in India in that lamentable condition, of "being without the knowledge of the true God, and Jesus Christ whom he hath sent," how ought it to stir up our minds to sympathise with their condition, and to give, cheerfully and liberally, "not grudgingly, or of necessity; for the Lord loveth a cheerful giver: and the liberal soul shall be made fat?"

CHAPTER XI.

January 29, 1814.—The detachments of invalids from Punamalee embarked at Madras on board the Marquis Wellington and Princess Charlotte of Wales. The Marquis Wellington, of nine hundred tons, wherein I was, received sixty of these invalids, *viz.* a party of the Royals, detachments from the 30th, 69th, 80th, 89th, and 25th light dragoons. We had very bad accommodation on board of this ship, having no less than sixteen sick men between each gun, many of whom could do nothing for themselves.

We had a long and very disagreeable passage; but I could have submitted to all the hardships attending the voyage much better, had it not been the dreadful wickedness that prevailed among us, as I shall have occasion to exemplify: but, indeed, this was the principal objection I had all along to the army; and it was the uncommon wickedness of my own regiment which rendered my other troubles less tolerable. But, to return to the children: when we embarked, an exact list of the names of the men was sent along with us; and when my name was called, and the children given in as belonging to me, the question was very naturally asked, Why is one of these children named Fleming, and the other Lee, when you are Serjeant B.? I related to them the story of the children in as few words as possible, all the time dreading lest they should not be permitted to go home with us; but the Lord, who has the "hearts of all men in his hand, and turns them as the rivers of water," gave us favour in the eyes of the Captain, who not only allowed them to go, but in a very short time after we sailed ordered his steward to give us regularly some broken meat after dinner. In this, he not only relieved the fatherless, but us also; for I generally received as much as sufficed both for my wife and myself. This was a great blessing; for, had I been obliged to take the ship's provisions, I certainly would have been at a great loss, considering my weak state of body, and the perpetual thirst to which I was subject. Here I thought I saw the blessing of God attending us for our kindness to the orphans. Here the Lord proved himself to be "a father to the fatherless," in putting it into our hearts to have compassion upon them; and, "when father and mother (in a certain sense) had forsaken them, then the Lord had thus taken them up."

I shall omit the greater part of my journal concerning this voyage; as there is a great variety of matter in which the reader could take no interest; such as our progress, the latitudes the ship reached at different dates—the number of torn sails, and broken yards—the dates of men's deaths, and to what regiments they belonged, &c. and notice a few circumstances which deeply interested me; and these I will state in nearly the same words as those in which they are inserted in my journal, that you may see how they affected me at the time, and to enable you better to understand what was my situation, and what sort of companions I had on board. I have noted down part of their discourse, just as it was uttered; and although you cannot be entertained, but rather shocked at the wickedness of man, and astonished at his depravity, yet the perusal may answer one good purpose; it may, by the blessing of God, render you more thankful that you are not compelled, as I was, to live among such monsters; but that you have a home, be it never so homely, and opportunity given you to read, meditate, and pray; that you have your Sabbaths and your ordinances; and, in a word, "That you can sit under your vines and fig trees, having none to make you afraid."

It was considerably against my comfort, while I was in this ship, that I was almost totally deprived of my wife's company; for a Captain Gordon of our regiment, who wished us both well, recommended her to a lady, whom she attended during the passage, and who paid her very handsomely for her trouble. This lady being in very delicate health, my wife was almost constantly employed in her cabin. I therefore had neither the pleasure of her company, nor much of her assistance in looking after the orphans; so that, I may say, I was both father and mother to them during the voyage.

March 20.—I see the Sabbath is always particularly pitched upon for wickedness of various kinds. I have thought that it was upon account of my taking more particular notice of what was going on, and having a greater desire to get myself composed for reading or serious reflection upon this day, that led me to think it worse employed than any other; but I perceive that I have been mistaken, for I find, upon a more careful examination, that upon the Lord's day these poor creatures seem as it were to think it a kind of unnecessary, as well as a disagreeable restraint put upon them; and that they therefore determine not to submit to it; and are resolved to make it appear that they are such brave fellows that God shall not restrain them; but, by their words, as well as their actions, say, "Our tongue is our own, who is lord over us? surely we will break his bands asunder, and cast away his chords from us."

This morning is introduced by swearing, obscene songs, abusing God's holy ordinances, and trampling upon his laws:—One man says, "Boys, get ready for drill;" another makes answer, "Drill, d———n! drill upon a Sunday;" a third begins an obscene song, painful upon any day to a modest ear; while a fourth says, "Leary, don't you know this is Sunday?" to which he makes answer, "Yes; and that his song was the text." This is certainly too much for me: I will go upon deck, and see if I can find any peace there; but when I went upon deck, there was one of our fine Scotsmen singing the "Blue Bells of Scotland," and the ship-officers pouring out the most horrid oaths against the seamen; while they, in return, were nothing behind, only in a lower tone, from fear of being heard. Oh, where shall I fly from these detestable beings, "whose throat is an open sepulchre, and whose mouth is full of cursing and bitterness!" This is my company upon the Lord's day; this is all I get for a sermon,—even cursing and swearing, obscene songs, and filthy communications. It is dreadful! I think, were there no other torments in hell but such society, there is an infinite cause of gratitude due to that compassionate Saviour, "who has delivered his people from it;"

but exercise patience, O my soul! consider that "the Lord knoweth how to deliver the godly out of temptations, as well as to reserve the unjust until the day of judgment, to be punished." I yet hope to have my Sabbaths and my ordinances. I yet hope to assemble with the people of God in his house of prayer, and, from a real experience, to say, "How amiable are thy tabernacles, O Lord of Hosts! my soul longeth, yea, even fainteth, for the courts of the Lord; my heart and my flesh crieth out for the living God," &c.

March 26.—Ten o'clock, P. M. One of the 30th Regiment departed this life. We have had a most alarming night of it, having a breeze right aft, and a sea running mountains high. It was necessary to support the masts with strong hawsers, to keep them from going over board. Upon the upper deck two of the carronades broke loose, with the smith's forge, and one of the pig styes; and upon the gun deck, all was a jumbled mass of confusion: the eighteen pound shot, foul water buckets, tins, tin-pots, salt beef, biscuit; with hats, knapsacks, red coats, and bags, knocking about among the salt water that was shipping down the hatchways. What with the noise of wind and waves above, and the rumbling and tumbling below, it was hardly possible to hear one another speak; and, when you add to all this, our being in pitch darkness *, you may see our situation was by no means enviable, but, on the contrary, very alarming and dangerous; yet these men could not forbear cursing and swearing, and flying in the face of him that could have sent us all to the bottom in a moment, ("and, O the infinite patience and forbearance of that God who did not!") I say, had we at this time gotten a watery grave, many of these hell-hardened creatures must have gone into the presence of their offended judge, blaspheming his holy

* We were allowed neither candle nor oil all the time we were on board; but we sometimes cut off a piece of the fat pork served out to us, and burned it in one of our iron canteen lids.

and reverend name. O what a dreadful state is it to be hardened in such a manner as to be unable to cease from this drudgery even for a single hour when awake, but to "be led captive by Satan at his will!" I have often thought, and it appears to me quite scriptural, that the wicked arrive at a state of far greater perfection in sin, and ripeness for hell in this world, than the people of God do in holiness and meekness for heaven, because they are the willing "servants of sin, and free from righteousness;" but the people of God carry about with them, while here, a "deceitful heart," which often betrays them into that "which their renewed natures abhor," and makes them cry out, "O wretched man!" But it is truly a happy consideration, that when the "earthly house of this tabernacle is dissolved," sin shall give us no more annoyance, for "we shall behold his face in righteousness, and shall be satisfied when we awake with his likeness," and shall inhabit that holy "house not made with hands, eternal in the heavens."

March 27.—The Psalmist says, in the cvii. Psalm, "They that go down to the sea in ships, and do business in the great waters; these see the works of the Lord, and his wonders in the deep, for he commandeth, and raiseth the stormy wind, which lifteth up the waves thereof; they mount up to the heavens, they go down again into the deep; they reel to and fro, and stagger like a drunken man." Surely they that are in such a situation, see much of the Almighty power of that glorious Being, "who holds the wind in his fist, and the waters in the hollow of his hand;" but in this ship, at least, we do not make a right improvement of such striking calls to heavenly contemplation; for we are this day viewing these wonderful displays of omnipotence, but appear to be as insensible to their language as the finny inhabitants of the great deep.

We had prayers read this day upon the quarter deck, which we heard with difficulty; but the sound was scarcely out of our ears, when some of our fine Scotsmen were at their old trade of cursing and swearing, whistling and singing, regardless both of the Lord's day, and the solemnity of his ordinances. I do not say but the men of other countries are fully as wicked; but I think it much more strange of Scotsmen; because, generally speaking, they receive better instruction, and have had a better example set before them in their youth; and, consequently, their sin is attended with many aggravations. But I hope the time will come, when I shall have it in my power to hear the Gospel preached, and be free from such depraved society; for "as the hart panteth after the water brooks, so panteth my soul after thee, O God! My soul thirsteth for God, for the living God; when shall I come and appear before God?"

April 3.—This is my birth-day; and I find it also to be the Sabbath, by the way it has been introduced. I shall here note down a specimen or two of the discourse

I am at present compelled to hear, that if it please the Lord to spare me to get out of this wicked place, where the works of darkness are carried on, and where the prince of darkness dwells, I may look at this, and remember my situation, and bless God for my deliverance. They are now talking of the different situations they are to hold when they go to h—ll. One says, he will be door-keeper; another, that he will be ferryman to row them over the river Styx; a third, that he is too bad for God, and he is sure that the Devil will have nothing to do with him; and, therefore, he must stand fast like the Old Buffs! But now they begin to blaspheme the "great and terrible name of God!" I will not write their awful expressions, but go out of the way a little, and, perhaps their discourse may be less shocking when I return; but I cannot expect much improvement while I am in this ship, because it is quite natural for them to speak in this way. For it is "out of the abundance of their heart that their mouth speaketh;" and they love to speak the language of hell, because it is their native country; and people are generally fond of speaking about the place they belong to.

April 8.—This is Good Friday I understand, by some of our strict religionists refusing to eat flesh. Yes, poor creatures, they are afraid of polluting themselves, although they can vomit up a belly-full of oaths without any remorse; and likewise trample upon every thing that is sacred. They are surely a sad compound of ignorance and superstition, for they do not consider that it is not that which entereth into a man that can defile him; but that which cometh out of him: these are the things which defile the man.

Early in the morning of the 10th of April we came in sight of the long-wished for island of St. Helena. This was a place which had been looked forward to with great eagerness by many in the ship besides myself, although the objects we had in view were, I doubt not, very different; for, so far as I am able to judge of my deceitful heart, the principal motive with me was the hope of seeing the Bengal and China fleets forward, as was generally expected, that we might not be detained waiting for them, but steer straight onward for Europe, and thus, by a prosperous voyage, I might be enabled sooner to leave these wicked scenes, and arrive the sooner at that happy country where the blessed streams of divine ordinances that make glad the city of our God flow in all their abundance. This was what I believe I eagerly coveted; my desires were, above all things, going out towards God, and towards the remembrance of his name; but I have every reason to believe the principal cause why many of my shipmates wished our arrival at St. Helena so intensely, was on account of their not having had it in their power, for a considerable time, to gratify a certain very strong propensity, produced by habit; or, in other words, there had raged amongst us, for some weeks, a famine of tobacco; the men had not counted on so tedious a passage to St. Helena, and, from this fatal mistake, they had not provided themselves with a sufficient stock before they came on board. The condition of many of these poor, miserable men, was indeed fitted to draw pity from all who knew from experience any thing of the amazing force of that desire, and take into account the present impossibility of getting it gratified, while, on the other hand, those who are free men, and not slaves to this lust, might be disposed to treat such people with contempt rather than sympathy, for being brought into such a miserably restless condition for the lack of an insignificant, unsightly leaf, and might think, if they had been in their circumstances, they would have thrown the pipe overboard, and have resolved against ever touching it again in their lives; but this is easier said than done, and this I know was a sacrifice which my unhappy shipmates found entirely too great to be accomplished.—No, to leave off smoking, and to cast away the pipe as a nuisance, was altogether out of the question; for smoke they must, although the appetite by which they were held in bondage compelled them to employ a strange and disgusting substitute for tobacco; for they had, for a number of days, been under the necessity of using a bit of tarry-rope yarn, in the form of oakum, with which they filled their pipes; and at that sickening stuff they would suck away until they were like persons in the rage of a fever, occasioned by the immoderate use of intoxicating liquors. We here see the great need there is for putting in practice the Apostle's resolution, "to beat under the body and keep it in subjection," that we may not be brought under the power of habits and practices, which, if not absolutely sinful in themselves, are almost sure to lead to much evil. This was, however, a great misery from which I was exempted; for although I had used tobacco for a series of years, my propensity to it by this time was completely abated. The reason of my giving up the use of tobacco was this :—Previously to our leaving Punamalee, I went to the doctor in charge of invalids, and told him I was afraid that smoking was unfavourable to my constitution, as it always excited a great palpitation at my breast, and a considerable desire to drink. He told me that if it produced such effects as I had described, it would be much better for me to give it up if I possibly could ; but added he was afraid that I would find it rather difficult, as it was a habit not easily overcome. However, I promised to take his advice, and accordingly the moment I entered the barracks, I gave all my sea-stock of pipes and tobacco to one of the men ; and by this one act, and the putting in full force the resolution I had formed, I was soon delivered from the desire itself, and was exempted from the dreadful effects of the present famine of that plant ; the want of which has caused so much uneasiness to individuals, and such great disturbances and privations in families; and which, in no small degree, drove on our unprincipled shipmates to curse father and mother, the day of their birth, and even that providence that had placed them in circumstances wherein it was impossible for them to obtain it. But although I was not in their state with regard to that tormenting desire, yet the intelligent Christian reader will easily perceive some resemblance between their condition and mine. The expedient to which they had recourse in the absence of tobacco, gave them considerably more pain than pleasure, and rather mocked and tantalized, than gratified their propensity.

In like manner, I may say, that in my attempts to get any spiritual consolation, I had more pain than profit; for when I set myself to read, meditate, or pray, I was sure to meet with some miserable opposition to distract my mind, which, perhaps, proved as great a trial to me as it would have been to one of these persons, at that time, to have had a pipe full of good tobacco snatched from his mouth, when he was in the act of enjoying it after his long abstinence. I use this similitude as I cannot find one upon the whole more suitable to represent my condition. They however had, on our arrival at St. Helena, considerably the advantage of me, for we were hardly well anchored when the idol of their hearts was presented to them; but, alas! it was far otherwise with me; for, to my great mortification, there seemed no great likelihood of my soon enjoying that happiness which "my soul was following hard after;" for, instead of the fleets being forward, there was only one outward-bound Indiaman lying in the bay. I see, therefore, O my soul! that there is nothing for it but patience; and, O Lord, grant that patience may have her perfect work, and let my present state of tribulation work patience, and a hope that will not make ashamed; and yet it is heart-breaking to think that I may be in this ship, and among these men, three months longer; but, O my soul, wait thou upon the Lord in the best way you can; be of good courage and he shall strengthen thine heart. Wait, I say, on the Lord. Commit thy way unto the Lord, trust also in him, and he shall bring it to pass. He shall even give thee the desire of thine heart.

April 20.—I was sent ashore to St. Helena this day, to bring two of our invalids on board. They received a pass until three o'clock yesterday, but did not return until I brought them from the main-guard, being confined for some misbehaviour ashore.

There was one of the 25th light dragoons died this day. We have had several deaths; but I mention this because of some circumstances attending it, as a further illustration of the character of those people amongst whom I dwell. I was amusing myself with a tune upon my violin, to drown the painful sound of that cursing and swearing which abounds, when one of the men interrupted me by saying, " Serjeant B——, don't you know that there is a man dying?" I answered, that " I did not know that he had been so ill." I went, therefore, immediately to see him, and found one of his comrades standing by the side of his hammock, attempting to comfort him in *his own* way. Another of his comrades, with a horrid curse, said, " Let him alone; let him sleep away, can't you?" But while he was yet speaking, the spirit of the dying man departed; and now they are beginning to enumerate all his good qualities, which, alas for him, were very few. One says he was a —— good fellow; another, he was a bloody good soldier; and a third, he was a h——h obliging fellow; and a fourth wished himself to be d——d if he should be thrown into the sea, for he would collect money in the ship to bury him ashore; while one of the former speakers declares, that he had prayed to God for him, and was sure he must now be happy. " Surely even the tender mercies of the wicked are cruel."—"My soul, come not thou into their secret, into their assembly mine honour be not thou united." I could have wished to have spoken to them about the absurdity, as well as the criminality of such conduct; but I knew that it would have had a bad effect, as it "would be giving that which is holy to dogs, and casting pearls before swine; and, therefore, they would no doubt have trampled them under their feet," and turned upon me with abusive language, and thus have sunk themselves deeper in guilt; so, upon a due consideration, I saw it to be my wisdom to keep "my mouth as with a bridle." But while I am yet writing, their temporary feelings of grief are over, and now they commence singing, and swearing, and arguing. Now from words they are coming to blows: I certainly must interfere, as being a part of my duty; but already the fight is over, and they are becoming more quiet. There is some disturbance upon deck: I will go and find out what is the cause. I have just learned, that the man who was talking so much about his prayers for the person just departed, was taken in the act of throwing himself overboard!—Poor creature, you are rescued from the jaws of death a little longer. But what can I expect from such men? He who infallibly knew "what is in man, and needed not that any should testify unto him," says that "a corrupt tree cannot bring forth good fruit."

April 23.—The dead man was interred this day upon the island; but it certainly would have been much better had he been thrown overboard in the usual manner; for the men, embracing the opportunity of getting ashore, where they could have plenty of liquor, returned at night drunk, and we had truly a dismal ship of it. It was no doubt insufferable at all times to a person who desired good order and quietness; but this night was by far the most dreadful we have experienced, for all the foul and detestable language that the devil and themselves could invent was brought forward; every thing that was horrid in cursing and swearing seemed to have been collected on this occasion; and their obscenity went so far as to expose their fathers and mothers in such a way as was shocking beyond conception. Had they really been begotten and born by the worst men and women that ever lived, it was impossible that they could have been guilty of what their vile children now laid to their charge. "But woe to the man that saith unto his father, what begettest thou? and to the woman, what hast thou brought forth?"

This was not all: One of them openly threatened to have blood for supper! and that lives should go for it before the morning, if the devil was alive, and as sure as God Almighty was ——! but I dare not venture to pollute my paper, or shock my readers, by reciting his expressions, which were only fit for the ears of men already in the place of everlasting torment. I had too much reason to think that my wife and I were the objects of his malice, and I did not know how to act. I knew that to confine him would only make matters worse when he should be released again; for he would then have some shadow of excuse for taking his revenge. His malice, as far as I knew, was entirely unfounded, for we had done him no harm, unless it was by conducting ourselves in a manner somewhat like what we ought to do; or because he saw us taken favourable notice of by the Captain, on account of the children. I therefore thought it would be our duty to remain upon deck, until the heat of his rage, and the heat of the liquor, were a little abated. But I found myself in too weakly a state of body to expose myself so long to the cold damp air, else I would have been inclined to this measure; for I saw, that to go below was attended with danger. After some deliberation, I resolved to commit myself and family to the care of the "keeper of Israel, who neither slumbers nor sleeps;" and we accordingly went to our hammocks, yielding ourselves wholly to the protection of our heavenly Father, in language similar to that of the Psalmist, when exposed to still more imminent dangers: "In thee, O Lord, do I put my trust; let me never be put to confusion. Deliver me in thy righteousness, and cause me to escape; incline thine ear unto me, and save me. Be thou my strong habitation, whereunto I may continually resort: thou hast given commandment to save me; for thou art my rock and my fortress. Deliver me, O my God, out of the hand of the wicked; out of the hand of the unrighteous and cruel man: for thou art my hope, O Lord God: thou art my trust from my youth. O Lord, be thou our hiding place; thou alone can preserve us from trouble;" and, in thy good time, O our God, do thou "compass us about with songs of deliverance."

We therefore lay down and slept quietly, because "the Lord made us to dwell in safety," even in the midst of danger. But after my first sleep, which was sweet, as my manner was, I arose to put the children to rights; and the first thing I laid my hand on, upon the top of my chest, was a razor fixed into a piece of wood, with a ring of lead round the handle; but my astonishment and terror were much increased, when I next found Mr. H., the man who had used the threatening language, lying upon the deck beside the chest, fast asleep. You may be sure I was not a little surprised to find matters in this state; for although I did suspect, and had great reason to suspect, that he intended us mischief, yet I partly persuaded myself, that after he had worn himself out with cursings, and threatenings of slaughter and vengeance, he would have become quiet, and forgotten us; but I now saw it to be otherwise: for here was a tolerably clear proof that he intended to carry his threats into execution against us when asleep; "but he that was for us, was stronger than all that were against us." Blessed be God, who delivered us from this "bloody and deceitful man." I thought it would be the best way to make no noise about it; and therefore threw the razor overboard, without even telling my wife the circumstance at the time, and returned again to my hammock, until gunfire. But, as a proof that my suspicions were well-founded, I must notice, that this razor never was inquired after. Had it belonged to any other of the men, there is little doubt but that they would have made a noise about it: and I would farther remark, that this man's conduct towards us was henceforth very different from what it had formerly been, being much more friendly during the time we remained in the ship.

May 19.—My mind was this day somewhat relieved, by the arrival of the China and Bengal fleets, as my hopes were excited that we would soon get out of the sight of these dreary rocks, which we had been looking upon, with sorrowful eyes, for these five weeks; but, to my sore mortification, I was again disappointed; for one of the frigates had suffered shipwreck the night before, by running against an Indiaman. The way it took place was this: The signal was given for the fleet to change their course; but the officer of the watch belonging to the merchant ship had either not been paying proper attention, or the hands had not been active enough in wearing their vessel round, and she still being upon her old tack, and the man of war upon the new direction, they ran foul of each other.—The frigate had her boltsprit, main-top, and top-gallant mast, fore-top, and top-gallant mast, carried away, and sprung her mizzen, so that she was altogether unmanageable; she had consequently to be towed into St. Helena by thirty of the boats belonging to the fleet, with her yards, sails, and masts, all hanging overboard;

and was really in the worst state ever I had seen a ship before. This was a bad concern both for them and us at the time; for we were anxious to get away, and they no doubt were very sorry for the damage they had received; but, upon account of this, we were all ordered to remain until she was refitted, which was in about a fortnight.

May 27. One of the men belonging to the 30th regiment died, and the last words I heard him utter, were a very common, but very dreadful imprecation; yet some of the survivors are saying, that it is well for him that he is gone, as if a person had no farther account to give; not considering that after death there is a judgment. Oh! what a vast difference there is between the death of the wicked, and that of the righteous; for "the wicked are driven away *in their wickedness*, but the righteous have hope in their death." It is truly lamentable to see men so hardened; nothing, it would seem, will be a warning to them; for, although this is the Lord's day, and one of their comrades is lying before them lifeless, yet are they playing at cards, whistling and singing, cursing and swearing alternately. O Lord, make me thankful for thy grace, make me thankful that thou hast not left me to the full force of my corruptions, to be carried away with them as with a flood; for what was I better than they? therefore I have nothing to glory of, because I have nothing but what I have received. "Not unto us, O Lord, not unto us, but unto thy name be the glory, for thy mercy and for thy truth's sake."

June 2. This is a happy day for some of us, for we are now moving towards home, and looking forward to see old Scotland once more. These feelings, together with the beautiful prospect of the fleet, consisting of fifty-one large ships, have an exhilarating effect upon the spirits. We had a serjeant of our regiment sent to the bottom this day in the usual form: which is, to sew up the person in his hammock, and to put a large shot or two at the feet to make him sink. When the corpse is prepared, it is carried upon deck, laid upon a grating, and covered with the union jack flag, and, after prayers are read over it in the English form, it is committed to the waves. It does not always sink immediately, for I have seen a dead body thrown over, in this way, move up and down like a bottle cast into a tub, as long as it was within our view, even when we were sailing at a very slow rate.

June 12. We crossed the equinoctial line this day. It is rather singular (as I found by my journal) that we crossed it on that very day seven years, on my voyage to India. If it please God, I hope I shall never cross it again.

It is now nineteen weeks since we left Madras. This Sabbath, as usual, is dreadfully profaned. I have been trying to read a little, to comfort myself, but I find it to be impossible, because of the wickedness by which I am surrounded; but lest I should become grievous to the reader by repeating the same things so often, I will, from this time, leave off any farther representations of this kind; and the reader may perhaps, from what I have already stated since I came on board of this ship, say, that I have been exhibiting an unfair and a too melancholy picture of man's depravity, and be apt also to say, or at least think, that if I were possessed of that Christian charity which thinketh no evil, I would hardly have said so much; and conclude, that I am some peevish, melancholy, uncharitable man; but judge not without proper evidence, "lest ye also be judged;" and take care that in judging me thou dost not "condemn thyself." Would to God I had not been able to say so much; had there been but one A. Chevis in the ship, how would it have cheered my spirits and repressed my complaints! for we could have borne one another's burdens: and it would have been far, very far, from me to have hid this "excellent one" from your view; but I have searched here with as anxious care to find a good man, as ever Solomon did to find a good woman, and unless I should be guilty of a lie, must declare, that I have not seen an individual amongst all those with whom I dwell, who does not habitually take the name of God in vain; and certainly you will not call these good men; for *this* is none of the spots of God's children, whatever "iniquities may prevail against them." I have informed the reader also that I had not the advantage of my wife's company, as she was always engaged in the cabin with her mistress. If he will then take all these circumstances into account, and attentively weigh them with an unprejudiced mind, I have no doubt but that he will be more disposed to pity than condemn me, seeing that I was doomed to six months of this dreadful society, which was worse to me than all my other hardships.

July 18. We have been becalmed for this fortnight past, and attended by a shark nearly all that time. It is rather singular, that I have always observed, both in my voyage to and from India, that we had always a death when this happened. I can give no rational account of this phenomenon, unless it be that the acute smell of this animal enables him to find out when there is sickness in a ship, and induces him to follow it in the hope of prey, when a body is thrown overboard. We have had a corpse thrown over this day, and will therefore soon be clear of our visitor. It is surprising that the shark can do such execution, if we consider the slenderness of his teeth, which resemble that of a saw, or rather a trap for catching rats; and they are generally provided with a double row of these, solid all round the jaw; but I have seen them nearly as thin as the main spring of a watch; yet he can cut through even bones with the utmost ease.

I shall give you an instance in proof of this assertion, which is the following:—The soldiers in India generally keep boys to carry their victuals, when on guard, or wash a pair of trowsers, or a shirt for them, if they run short before the washerman comes with their clothes: and when we lay in Madras, (where by the bye we could get young sharks to buy in the bazaar, as we do *speldings* in this country, at a halfpenny each,) one of these boys, after having washed his master's clothes, went into the sea to bathe, while they were drying; and, being a good swimmer, he ventured beyond the surf, when a shark perceiving him, whipt off his leg, in half the time one of our anatomists would have done it with his saw. But this is not the most affecting part of the story; for although the poor little fellow had lost his leg, and with great difficulty reached the shore, leaving the water, as he came along, tinged with blood, he, in his dying moments, told his comrades who were upon the beach with him, where his master's clothes were lying, and desired that they would take them safe to the barracks: medical assistance was immediately called, but before the surgeon could reach the place, his spirit was fled. It is remarkable that these fish, when they are in pursuit of their prey, admit their young, in the same manner as some species of the serpent do, into a cavity of their belly, which God, in his wonder-working providence, has provided for their reception. In proof hereof, when we were going to India, one of the sailors, having out his shark line at the stern of the vessel, which is generally done when they observe this fish following, he hooked a very large one, and hauled it into the ship, by a tackle from the end of the main-yard; and after having the fish fairly on board, one of the sailors took a large hatchet, with which he cut off its head; and to the no small alarm of the bare-footed soldiers, who made the best of their way off in all directions, out sprung no less than eleven young sharks, tumbling and gaping about the deck, to the great danger of all feet and toes within their reach. Some of these young ones were three feet long. The sailors very frequently eat this fish, on account of its being fresh; and this one was accordingly cut into junks, (as they call it,) and divided among the crew. I tasted, through curiosity, a little bit of it, which had a very strong disagreeable flavour; but the very idea of them devouring human flesh, is enough to make one shudder, although their taste should excel that of the finest turtle. I would further observe, that the shark does not give his teeth much trouble in chewing his food, for we took another the same day, which had a six pound piece of beef in his belly, not the least macerated; and the tally* of the

* The tally is a piece of wood, with the number of the mess to which it belongs marked upon it. These are used on board a ship, to distinguish between the pieces of meat,—for without something of this kind, it would be impossible for one mess to know its own.

mess to which the beef belonged, still tied to it with a string.

July 24.—We saw one of the Western Islands upon our starboard bow—we saw also two strange sail, supposed to be American privateers; our frigates and gun brigs went in chace immediately, but they have not returned to the fleet as yet. We have a very stiff breeze, and a heavy sea, and have shipped a wave just now which has swept some of the men off the hatchway.

July 29.—We have had a heavy gale these three days and nights, but the worst of it is, the wind is almost right a-head; and we consequently have made very little way. The children have been in their hammock all that time without light, except when the men occasionally lighted a bit of fat pork (as I said they sometimes did) to eat their victuals; and when I took them upon deck they were like new started hares, and jumped and ran about until I was obliged to restrain them from fear of their driving themselves against the sides of the ship.

Aug. 4.—A large boat is come along side of us from Torbay upon chance, to take away *certain* goods from the passengers. I spoke to one of the boatmen, who told me that we are about thirty miles from land, and two of the sailors have been sent to the mast head to look out for it; we have also received our pilot, and are running about nine knots an hour. Truly this is delightful; and I trust, that he who has preserved us hitherto, will bring us in "safety into the desired haven."

Aug. 11.—We have had considerable difficulty in getting up the river, on account of the wind being contrary; but we are now safe moored, and they are beginning to take out the guns to lighten her, that they may be able to get her up to Blackwall. There is an order just come for us to go ashore to-morrow. Joyful news, to think of getting out of this miserably wicked place! how it enlivens my

N 6

spirits besides to view the fields of corn, and the cattle feeding by the sides of the river, particularly when it is, I may say, my native country! O, what time brings about; for I have often almost despaired of ever seeing it; and, although I am now a poor feeble creature, hardly able to crawl, yet as Solomon says, "while we are joined to all the living there is hope; for a living dog is better than a dead lion;" and I bless God, that I am "the living, the living to praise him," while hundreds of my comrades are rotting upon a foreign shore.

Aug. 12.—We got all safe ashore at Chelsea, which place was completely crowded with invalids from the Continent, besides those from India; they were in all about four thousand. The Tower and Chelsea being full, some hundreds were billetted in the country. This promised very badly with regard to pension, and upon the 14th of September, 1814, the day on which I passed, there were several hundreds who did not get a penny. I, however, received ninepence, which, after all, was but a small recompense for all my hardships, and their bad effects upon my constitution, and a service of fourteen years in the 26th, and Royals together; but had it not been that I was so long Serjeant and Fife-Major of the latter regiment, I would not have received more than sixpence. I desire to be thankful, however, for this allowance; although it be small, it is always something to look to.

CHAPTER XII.

I SHALL not trouble the reader with a particular account of the various occurrences that came under my notice while we lay at Chelsea, which was about five weeks: such as, the great difficulty we had in obtaining a lodging; the many wonderful things to be seen about London; the behaviour of the invalids; to what regiments they belonged, &c. But there is one thing which I think it would certainly be wrong to omit, because it is illustrative of the loving-kindness of the Lord, whose glory we ought to have in view in all that we do.

While I was in this place I found one of my brothers working at Vauxhall bridge, who was one of Mr. Fletcher of the Secession's hearers. My wife and I, therefore, upon the first sabbath after we went ashore, accompanied him to Miles's Lane Chapel, and heard a Mr. M'Donald, I think, who was officiating in the absence of Mr. F. at this time in Scotland. Upon entering the meeting house, a mixture of unutterable reverence and joy thrilled through my soul, while I thought of the solemnity of the place, and looked back on the long dreary period during which I had been deprived of an opportunity of "assembling with the people of God in his house of prayer." But how was I struck with adoring wonder, when the preacher gave out the 63d psalm,

"Lord, thee my God, I'll early seek:
My soul doth thirst for thee," &c.

which he prefaced in a very pathetic manner; and during the whole of the explanation, set forth the Psalmist's condition, so exactly applicable to the feelings and circumstances of my past life, particularly in

India and in my voyage home; and the next psalm which he gave out was the 122d,

> "I joyed when to the house of God,
> Go up, they said to me," &c.

which was equally applicable to my now happy situation. I found it too much for my feelings, for I thought my heart would have burst with alternate joy and sorrow. Joy, when I saw in this the answer of many a longing desire, "and my prayers returned into mine own bosom;" and sorrow, because of the many unbelieving and ungrateful thoughts I had formerly entertained, that "I should never again see the Lord, even the Lord, in the land of the living," until a flood of concealed tears gave me some relief; and a sweet believing tranquillity took the place of these conflicting passions. The whole of the services of the day corresponded with its commencement, and all had a tendency to refresh and satisfy my thirsty soul, more than the vernal showers of the east could cheer and invigorate the face of languishing nature; and I do trust they "did not return to the Lord void, but prospered in that thing whereunto they were sent." Surely the Psalmist's choice of spending his time was mine, for I certainly esteemed "this day better than a thousand," and found these comforts sweeter to my soul than honey to my mouth. Surely on this happy day, if ever in my life, I found out in a great measure the truth and emphasis of these gracious words: "Blessed are they which do hunger and thirst after righteousness, for they shall be filled." But, I trust, my dear reader, you will excuse me, when I tell you that I am unable to describe my emotions at this time. However, if you are one of those persons spoken of by the apostle, who "have their senses exercised to discern both good and evil," you can better enter into my state than I am able to inform you; although you cannot be expected to feel to the same degree as

I have felt, unless you had suffered, to the same extent, as I have suffered. But if you are really one "of Christ's scholars, and taught by his Holy Spirit, that Spirit dwells in you," and "he will teach you in some measure his own language," and you will know something of what is meant by "the soul being satisfied with marrow and fatness," of the Lord lifting upon his people "the light of his countenance," of causing his face to shine upon them;" and of "his loving kindness being better than life."—You will know something of "the joy of the Lord," the "joy of God's salvation," and "the joy of the Holy Ghost," "of being filled with all joy and peace in believing;" &c. but if these, and the like passages, be to you an unknown tongue, or a language which you do not understand, I am afraid that you have the alphabet of Christianity to learn yet, and "have need that one teach you over again, which be the first principles of the oracles of God; and are indeed among such as have need of milk, and not of strong meat." All that I shall say more upon this subject is, that I found this place to be a Bethel, for surely the Lord was there, for it was to me none other than the house of God, surely it was to me the very gate of heaven.—O taste, and ye shall find also that the Lord is good; and that the man is truly blessed which trusteth in him.

You may be sure we did not remain long in Chelsea, after I passed the board; for I went immediately to Millar's wharf, and found there a vessel bound for Leith. I therefore took our passage in the steerage; but I had cause afterwards to repent that I did not take a cabin passage, for the steerage was so completely stowed with baggage, that all the passengers were obliged to lie upon deck the whole way; this was a mischievous bath, for us particularly, who had just come from India, considering that it was in the month of September.

On landing at Leith we put our baggage into a cart, and went off to Pennycuick immediately, where we were joyfully received; we remained there with our friends a few days, after having been nearly eleven years absent, and having only seen them once during that period, when I visited them, on furlough, from Ireland.

After we had recruited ourselves, we were anxious to get the children settled before I thought of settling myself; and we accordingly went with them to Edinburgh, and took tickets on the outside of the Glasgow coach. When we arrived at that place, we immediately went to Anderston, and found out the dwelling of William Stevenson, the grandfather, on the mother's side, of Serjeant Lee's child. The old folks received us with great expressions of gratitude, on account of what we had done for the poor, destitute orphans of their deceased daughter. The neighbours also came flocking in, to behold the children who were born in such a far distant land; and expressed their astonishment at the way which the providence of God had taken to bring them home, considering that we were in no wise related to any of them. They wrote off to Serjeant Fleming's father, who lived at Kilmarnock, and he no sooner received the intelligence, than he came off to Anderston, accompanied by one of his sons, and when we were all assembled, we spent a very happy day together.

After remaining some time in their company, giving and receiving information, we bethought ourselves of returning home. So Mr. Fleming took the child of his deceased son, and the little girl of the deceased Serjeant Lee remained in Anderston: but Mr. Stevenson, and his wife being old, and apparently very infirm, we told them, that if it was the will of God to remove either of them by death, and in consequence thereof the child should become burdensome to the survivor, or might herself be neglected, that we would still consider ourselves as parents to the child, and do for her in every respect as if she were our own ; and requested them, moreover, to be sure to keep up a correspondence with us by letters.

It was not many months after this when I received the news of the old man's death. According to promise, I therefore went from Peebles to Anderston, to bring home the little girl, who still recollected me, calling me *daddy* when ever I entered the house, and attempted to wash my feet, which were very sore by marching a good way that morning. I stopped a day to rest myself, and during that time she would not allow me to be out of her sight, neither could any of her uncles or aunts induce her to go with them anywhere unless I desired her. I thought it would be my best plan, both for expedition and on account of the child, to take a ticket in the coach: so I acted accordingly. When we reached Edinburgh, I went to a house, head of the Candlemaker Row, and found there a return-chaise for Peebles, at which I was very happy, and we set off as soon as the driver was ready, as I was anxious to get home. We arrived safe at Peebles about eleven o'clock at night; but, when I knocked at the door, which my wife had just shut, preparing for bed, she could hardly believe that I could have so soon returned. But, when she saw her poor little dear, as she called her, she took her in her arms, and embraced her with all the symptoms of an affectionate mother who had been robbed of her innocent, that was now again restored to her arms, her bosom, and her affections.

Now, my dear reader, this is what became of the orphans, and who knows but God, whose "way is in the sea, and whose path is in the great waters;" may intend this poor little Indian orphan to sooth our dying bed, and to be our greatest earthly friend, when a true friend is valuable.—

While we were in Peebles, I tried my old occupation of working at the loom; but I was compelled to leave it off, as this employment would not agree with my constitution, being much afflicted with a pain in the breast, and a giddiness in my head; which were truly distressing.

We had not lived long in Peebles after the child came to us, when I received a letter directed, Serjeant B——, Peebles, late of the Royal Scots. When I looked at the back of the letter, I could not understand who was the writer, yet I thought the hand familiar; but when I opened it, to my great astonishment I found it to be from Colonel Stewart, saying that he had just learned that I was returned from India in a very bad state of health, which he was very sorry for; and said, moreover, that if he could be of any service in procuring any situation suitable for me, he would be happy to do it, and likewise expressed a desire to see me. I accordingly went to his country seat near Stirling, where he had just gone; and, after many kind inquiries upon both sides, he asked me if I could point out any thing that he or his interest could do for me. I expressed my gratitude in the best way I could for his kind offer, but told him that I could think of nothing but a drum-major's situation in a local militia corps, though at the same time I said, that I was afraid that it would be difficult to be obtained; but it did not appear so to him, and he hoped that he would soon be able to procure it. He desired me to remain all night, and gave his servants particular charge to pay all possible attention to my comfort.

I had not returned to Peebles above three weeks, when I received a letter from this kind friend, informing me that he had obtained a situation for me in the Greenock Local Militia; and I accordingly went and took the charge of that corps the following week: but there is nothing in this world to be depended on; for I had not enjoyed my new situation, in which I received half-a-guinea weekly, above six months, when an order came for the staffs of these regiments to be broke. But Colonel Stewart again voluntarily befriended me, for he recommended me, previous to this taking place, to the notice of his brother, at this time bailie of Greenock, who fell upon a plan for assisting me. The gentlemen of Greenock had often expressed a wish for a billiard-table, that they might amuse themselves at a vacant hour; and Mr. Stewart having a room suitable for the purpose, agreed to fit it up as a billiard-room, if I would take the situation of marker to the billiard-table. I told him I would be very happy to do it, but that it was an affair with which I was entirely unacquainted; but he said that it was very easily learned, and that I would soon be master of the business. I accordingly took the charge of this room; for which I received a very equitable reward.

I had not been long in my new situation, when I understood my duty pretty well; and observing that I would have much spare time, I wished to turn it to some good account. I therefore made inquiry at a very intelligent acquaintance, if he could inform me where I could get a book that contained portions of Scripture, arranged under different heads, as I wished to write them out, and thereby get better acquainted with the contents of my Bible: and by this employment might at once be both amused and instructed. So he recommended Dr. Chalmers's "Scripture References," telling me, that it was the very kind of book I was seeking. I went and procured it immediately; and I did not let much time pass, until I commenced writing out, in full, the passages referred to by the Doctor; but when I came to that head, "Duties under Affliction," how agreeably was I surprised, when I found, under it, that blessed passage which gave me so much relief and comfort in the Prince of Wales' Island, "Call upon me in the day of trouble; I will deliver thee: and thou shalt glorify me."

The reader may be rather surprised that I never before this hour had seen these precious words, and maybe apt to draw, not unfairly, this conclusion, that "if I had read my Bible much, I certainly would have seen this delightful promise before now." I do freely acknowledge that I have not read my Bible with that attention and frequency I might have done, and ought to have done, though I have, upon the whole, endeavoured to make myself acquainted with it by frequent reading; but, by not going regularly through it, I had never happened to meet with the above passage, although it was now fully ten years since it was a mean, in the hand of the spirit which dictated it, of "turning for me my mourning into dancing, and girding me with gladness." After I was finished, therefore, with the scripture references, and not being yet tired with this pleasant labour, I added other three parts to my intended Pocket

Companion, *viz.* a Selection of Passages from Mr. Henry's Method for Prayer; an Explanation of the Principal Religious Terms from Mr. Brown's Dictionary of the Bible; and Extracts from Mr. M'Ewan's Essays. When these four parts were finished, I had the whole bound together into a pretty sizeable volume, the substance of which I intended to commit to memory. But I had not finished this work many days, when Mr. W——, our minister, came to see us, as he frequently did, and asked me what I had been doing this long time, that I had never given him a call. I told him how I had been employed. He expressed a desire to see what I had been writing, and I showed him the book. After he had examined it a little, he asked me if I would allow him to peruse it for a few days? I said, he was perfectly welcome to do that. When he had done so, he came back to our house with the book, and expressed his satisfaction with regard to the usefulness and conciseness of the compilation; and told me that it was an excellent work, (if I could think of publishing it,) for the instruction of servants, seamen, and even the greater part of the labouring classes, who had little time to peruse, or money to purchase books, where those useful subjects were set forth more at large, and above all, that it might be unspeakably useful to assist or to prepare people who were lately, or about to be married, in their family devotions and instructions. I at first could upon no account think of consenting to his request; but I told him that I would consider about it a few days. He returned in a short time afterwards to know my determination. I said that I would be very happy to publish the book, if I really thought it would be useful to my fellow men, particularly as I had as much money by me as would pay for printing a few hundred copies; but I said also, that I was ashamed of my name being affixed to a printed book, even though it was a compilation. This objection, however, he obviated, by stating, that it might be published without a name; and, in short, having brought matters thus far, he went and made a bargain with a printer; and after the impression was thrown off, he recommended it very warmly from the pulpit, and not only he, but two other clergymen, also recommended it in strong language, particularly to servants and seamen. In consequence of all this, I either sold or gave away the whole impression in little more than a twelvemonth.

We remained in Greenock until the year 1820, at which time both duty and inclination seemed to call us to Edinburgh, on account of my old parents, who resided there, and were, at this period, in a very poor state of health; that we might try if we could do any thing for the comfort of them who could now scarcely do any thing for themselves; while their other children were unable to afford them much relief, on account of their numerous families. Another weighty motive for my removal was, that I would there have an opportunity of consulting a very able physician, with whom I was well acquainted, as he had been assistant surgeon* in our regiment all the time I was in India, whom I knew to understand perfectly my constitution, and the many and severe attacks it had sustained, from different disorders, while in that country, which had rendered a once healthy bodily frame, now almost totally useless; for I had enjoyed a very indifferent state of health ever since my sore illness in Trichinopoly. The person to whom I allude was Dr. B——, a gentleman whose indefatigable and successful labours, in ascertaining the nature and cure of the diseases of hot climates, for the benefit of the men under his charge, are well known to every man in the regiment.

* This medical officer left our regiment, being promoted to the rank of head surgeon to his majesty's 33d regiment; and, at this time, was practising for himself in Edinburgh.

I therefore left Greenock at the Whitsunday term, and finding myself still in the same delicate state, I went to Dr. B——, who received me with great expressions of kindness. He inquired very particularly into every circumstance with regard to my health since I left India; which gave me an opportunity of relating the various modes of treatment which had been prescribed to me by different medical men to whom I had applied without finding any permanent benefit. After having satisfied all his inquiries as well as I could, he said that he was afraid that their mode of treatment was calculated rather to do harm than good, but that he would call at my lodgings in a day or two. He accordingly came most punctually; and, after having made all due inquiry for ascertaining the true nature of my complaint, he told me that my liver was in a very bad state, and that he would strongly recommend me to submit to a course of mercury, &c. With this proposal I readily complied; and, having undergone that course of treatment which his superior skill thought proper to administer, I derived unspeakable benefit from it. A short time after I was able to go abroad with safety, I went to his house, at his desire, and called upon him, to let him know how well I was coming on. I was also, no doubt, anxious by this time to know the amount of his bill, which, I thought must be considerable, when I took into the account his own personal attendance, for about nine weeks; but how was my astonishment excited, when he told me that, as I was an old fellow-traveller, and brother soldier, the amount of my bill was nothing; but that I was perfectly welcome to all that he had done for me; and, moreover, that he would be very happy to serve me, or my family, at any time when medical attendance was necessary.

I confess I am unable, my dear reader, to express, in words, a proper sense of this gentleman's kindness; I therefore think it the best way of manifesting my gratitude, by being silent, and desiring that the generous reader would place himself, as it were, in my situation, and try what he would think or feel upon such an occasion: but this I will say, that I have, since the time referred to, enjoyed a better state of health than ever I have had these nine years past, and I trust I will carry the grateful remembrance of Dr. B.'s beneficial benevolence to my last hour.

There is just one other circumstance that I will mention, as it is rather singular, and then come to a conclusion. After I settled in Edinburgh, there was a meeting of our family, consisting of eight children, all being present on this occasion but one, who was a mason in England. Now it is somewhat remarkable, that of these now present, four had been but a little time before scattered very widely all over the world. My oldest brother at that time belonged to the artillery, and was in America; I myself, who am next in the order of time, was in India; the third was in Spain with the 94th, having been engaged in all the actions to which that gallant regiment was called; the last and youngest of the four, was in Ireland, with the Renfrewshire militia; yet, by the kind providence of God, our aged parents saw us now all under one roof; all out of the army, each rewarded according to his various services, and all settled in a way of doing, in or near Edinburgh, each of us according to our ability at this time engaging to add to their future comfort, which you cannot doubt made them a happy couple, and you need not wonder at them adopting language similar to that of the ancient and venerable Patriarch, when his son Joseph was restored to his embraces in safety, after he had long lost all hope of his being in life: "Now Lord let us die in peace, since we have seen our children's faces, and because that they are yet alive."

My wife has still retained an excellent state of health, notwithstanding all her former hard marches, being blessed with one of the best constitutions I have ever known any woman possessed of; and the poor little invalid that cost her so much nursing, is also a very fine healthy child. The other child, who went to Kilmarnock, we have heard lately is also in perfect good health. My wife's daughter, who came to us in Greenock, is also quite well, and still forms a part of our little family. "Bless the Lord, O my soul, and forget not all his benefits." And when I consider all the way that the Lord our God has led us, for so many years in the wilderness, I am here disposed, with Jacob, to set up my monument of gratitude with this inscription—

"HITHERTO THE LORD HATH HELPED US."

FINIS.

www.ingramcontent.com/pod-product-compliance
Lightning Source LLC
Chambersburg PA
CBHW062036090426
42740CB00016B/2926

* 9 7 8 1 5 3 5 8 0 7 7 3 9 *